TUSCALOOSA, ALABAMA
REGISTERED ARCHITECT

The Three Prejudices

by Kelley Varner

© Copyright 1997 — Destiny Image Publishers

All rights reserved. This book is protected under the copyright laws of the United States of America. This book may not be copied or reprinted for commercial gain or profit. The use of short quotations or occasional page copying for personal or group study is permitted and encouraged. Permission will be granted upon request. Unless otherwise identified, Scripture quotations are from the King James Version of the Bible. Scriptures marked NIV are from the New International Version. NIV. Copyright, 1973, 1978, 1984 by International Bible Society. Scriptures marked (TLB), (ASV), (NKJ), and (AMP) are taken from The Living Bible, the American Standard Version, the New King James Version, and the Amplified Bible, respectively. Scripture quotes are also taken from the Moffatt, Phillips, Weymouth, and Jerusalem Bible translations as indicated.

Take note that the name satan and related names are not capitalized. We choose not to acknowledge him, even to the point of violating grammatical rules.

Destiny Image® **Publishers, Inc.**
P.O. Box 310
Shippensburg, PA 17257-0310

"Speaking to the Purposes of God for This Generation
and for the Generations to Come"

ISBN 1-56043-187-3

For Worldwide Distribution
Printed in the U.S.A.

First Printing: 1997   Second Printing: 1999

This book and all other Destiny Image, Revival Press,
and Treasure House books are available
at Christian bookstores and distributors worldwide.

For a U.S. bookstore nearest you, call **1-800-722-6774**.
For more information on foreign distributors, call **717-532-3040**.
Or reach us on the Internet: **http://www.reapernet.com**

Dedication

To all who have had a burden for reconciliation and unity in the Body of Christ.

Acknowledgments

To Don Nori, for helping to birth this book. His courage and insightful wisdom have been a constant strength to me.

To Dr. Fuchsia Pickett, Bishop Earl P. Paulk, and Dr. Michael Brown, for their exemplary lives and ministries that have paved the way for unity in the Body of Christ. Thank you for your kind words and support.

About the Cover

I approach all cover designs the same way: I read some of the manuscript; then I pray to find out what God wants to show through the cover. As I prayed over this cover, God reminded me of one of my favorite worship songs—"Break Dividing Walls" by David Ruis. I saw the walls of racism, gender, nation. Then suddenly, I saw a sledgehammer smash into the walls, causing them to shatter. I knew that was what I had to show. I was later told (after the cover design was completed and presented to the author) that Pastor Varner had once received a prophecy that he would be a sledgehammer to break down spiritual walls. What a confirmation! Praise God, the walls are coming down!

Tony Laidig

Table of Contents

Preface

Preface

Prejudice...

Prejudice is anything that separates us from God and each other.

Prejudice is learned behavior. Men have discovered how to build all kinds of walls.

Prejudice is hate, and it is based upon the spirit of fear. Its underlying essence is insecurity— the fear of rejection, of not being accepted.

Prejudice is "pre-judgment," an opinion formed before the facts are known. It is unreasonable bias.

Prejudice is bigotry, discrimination, intolerance, narrow-mindedness, opinion, partiality. Prejudice is poison.

Prejudice is the innate, corrupted character of the old Adamic nature that causes men to choose whom they love.

Prejudice has to do with character, the heart condition of the inner man.

Prejudice is engrained in us. It is that thing that knots up in our gut and really upsets us when we hear the truth. Prejudice pushes our buttons and rings our bell.

Prejudice can never be surmounted by human means. The only real, lasting cure for this unholy spirit is the love of God. The single antidote for this spirit of antichrist is the supernatural, dynamic, life-changing power of the Holy Spirit.

The only remedy for this universal human need is the personal and collective experience of the love of God—being forgiven, accepted in the Beloved, safe and secure in Christ.

Simply stated, *prejudice* is "pre-judgment."

It is taken from the Latin *praejudicium*, which is made up of two words: *prae*, which means"before"and *judicium*, which means "a judgment." *Webster's Dictionary* defines *prejudice* as:

1. A judgment or opinion formed before the facts are known; preconceived idea, favorable or, more usually, unfavorable.

2. A judgment or opinion held in disregard of facts that contradict it; unreasonable bias.

3. The holding of such judgments or opinions.

4. Suspicion, intolerance, irrational superstition or hatred of other particular races, creeds, regions, occupations, religions, etc.

5. Injury or harm resulting as from some judgment or action of another or others.

Some synonyms of "prejudice" are "bias, bigotry, chauvinism, detriment, discrimination, distortion, inclination, injustice, intolerance, jaundice, narrow-mindedness, one-sidedness, opinion, partiality, partisanship, poison, preconception, prejudgment, prepossession, racism, sexism, subjectivity, unfairness." [1]

The Scriptures clearly show "prejudice" to be part of the innate, corrupted character of the old Adamic nature that causes men to choose whom they love. Prejudice has to do with character, the heart condition of the inner man.

Three great prejudices have infested the homes, churches, businesses, and cities of our society:

1. Gender (the walls between men and women).

2. Race (the walls between blacks and whites [and all other skin colors]).

3. Nation (the walls between Jews and Gentiles).

These walls can never be surmounted by human means. The people of God have fostered these ills through ignorance and apathy. We must repent and receive an adjusted vision. Our only hope is enlightenment and the Spirit-directed action of His Church, as salt and light, as one nation under God and His Word.

These man-made fences are spiritual as well as natural predicaments. Mere human genius will never warm the chilly climate created by these controversies. The fire of the Holy Spirit, the same Spirit that raised Jesus Christ from the dead, must breathe upon these cold, dry bones.

We need a revival of the love of God. There are different Greek words for *love*. *Eros* describes love between men and women, a kind of love that can be experienced without the Holy Spirit. *Phileo* describes the love between friends, a quality of love that can be experienced apart from God's anointing. However, *agape*, divine love, the love of God—the reverse side of prejudice—must be poured out into men's hearts by the Holy Ghost.

The only real, lasting cure for the unholy spirit of prejudice is the love of God. The single antidote for the spirit of antichrist is the supernatural, dynamic, life-changing power of the Holy Spirit.

The New Testament biblical name for this divine Spirit is *Christ*, which means, "the anointed One."

Jesus of Nazareth, the Head of the Church, has become both Lord and Christ. Since His death and resurrection, Jesus has bestowed upon all flesh His Spirit, the Holy Spirit, the Spirit of the Son. As Christians, we are His Church, the Body of Christ. Together, we comprise the fullness of Him who fills all things.

"Christ," the new nature of the new man, is not prejudiced. "Christ" transcends time and space. He has been exalted above every fear, living in the realm of faith. Wars and all walls between the sexes, races, and nations are beneath Him.

Gal. 3:28, KJV

There is neither Jew nor Greek, there is neither bond nor free, there is neither male nor female: for ye are all one in Christ Jesus.

In Christ, there is neither male nor female. In Christ, there is neither bond nor free. In Christ, there is neither Jew nor Greek. We are one in Christ Jesus, born from above. We have become a new creation—a new species without gender, a heavenly race, a spiritual nation, a divinely elected ethnicity.

We are all impacted daily by these three great problem areas—prejudice of gender, race, and nation. Too many preachers have become politicians, afraid to tackle the hard questions. "Seeker sensitive" churches and the obsession to be politically correct are the order of the day. We have sodden, or watered down, the gospel of the Lamb. We have mastered the art of practicing "safe church."

Consider the following issues: Can a woman preach the gospel? Should she be allowed to teach men? Are there female apostles and bishops? What contributions have women made throughout Church history? Did Eve bring sin into the world? Should women wear head coverings? Is the woman's place in the home?

Was Ham cursed with black skin? Is this the day of the black man? What does the Bible say about interracial marriages? Are there notable people of color in the Bible? Was Jesus black?

Who is the real Jew? Who are the heirs of the Palestinian covenant? Will God pour out His Spirit on natural or spiritual Israel? What is the gospel of the Kingdom? How should we interpret Romans 9–11?

Prepare your heart and mind to explore with me the reality of the Scriptures, which will be corroborated by the record of history. There are answers to each of these questions that make real spiritual and intellectual sense.

I have written this book as a prophet, not a teacher. My aim has been to boldly proclaim truth to the end that we all might work with God toward His ultimate intention as He gathers all things to Himself in Christ. Our foundation, our beginning point, is enough: We are all one in Christ Jesus. And *He* is not prejudiced!

Kelley Varner, B.S., Th.B., D.D.
Senior Pastor, Praise Tabernacle
Richlands, North Carolina

Part One

The Walls That Divide

"…and hath broken down the middle
wall of partition…."

Ephesians 2:14

Chapter One

Christ Is Not Prejudiced

"...to live is Christ...."

Philippians 1:21

There are only two types of men on planet Earth, Christ and Adam. The Scriptures reveal these two natures as the new man and the old man, beauty and the beast.

Christ loves everyone. Adam is full of bigotry and bias. Christ is from above. Adam is from below. Christ is awake, having risen to newness of life. Adam is asleep, dead in trespasses and sins. Christ is the wisdom of God. Adam grovels about in darkness and ignorance. Christ is the power of God. Adam is a cowardly wimp.

The Bible portrays these two kinds of hearts with a number of pictures—wheat and tares, sheep and goats, light and darkness, saints and sinners. Neither nature has any basis in gender, race, or nationality.

These two starkly contrasted spirits are pictured in the Old Testament by Abel and Cain, Abraham and Nimrod,

Isaac and Ishmael, Israel and Esau, Samuel and Eli, David and Saul, Elijah and Ahab. Eventually both spirits are personified in one person, the New Testament Paul, who was first Saul of Tarsus.

These diverse figures also typify the contrast between these natures: Sarah and Hagar, Rachel and Leah, Ruth and Naomi, Abigail and Michal, Esther and Vashti. Each of these dichotomies illustrates the principle of the "freewoman and the bondwoman" of Paul's famous allegory in Galatians 4:21-31.

The Epistle to the Galatians also reveals the starting point for overcoming prejudice; *Christ* is revealed as a "seed," a *spiritual* seed (Jn. 1:1-4; Gal. 3:16,19,29; 1 Pet. 1:23). The new nature has nothing to do with gender, race, or nationality. That divine seed is neither male nor female; we are one race from among the races, and one nation from among the nations!

This "en-Christed" seed is *spiritual*! *Nature* and *character* are therefore at the root of all prejudice. The Bible plainly teaches that Christ is "the image of God," and Jesus Christ is the "express image" of the Father's Person (2 Cor. 4:4; Heb. 1:3). This Greek word is *charakter*, and it means "engraving (['character'], the figure stamped, an exact copy or representation)." *Charakter* can also mean "a stamp or impress."

Christians are to be conformed to the *image* of Jesus. We have put on the new man, renewed in knowledge after the image of Him who created us. Believers are to put on and wear as a garment the image of the heavenly. This glorious work of His Spirit transforms us from one degree of glory to another. Our blessed hope is to be like

Him. Those who are pure in heart focus on God, not gender, race, or nationality.

Again, God's seed is a *spiritual* seed. This truth can be expounded by developing these four essential truths:

1. Christ is the new nature, the new creation Man.

2. Christ is transcendent.

3. Christ is altogether new.

4. Christ is not prejudiced—He is not divided.

Christ Is the New Nature, the New Creation Man

The Hebrew word *Messiah* is equivalent to the Greek word *Christ*; each means "the anointed one." The Anointed One of the New Testament is both Head and Body, constituting one new creation Man.[1]

First and foremost, the glorious Head of that new unified Man is Jesus of Nazareth, the uniquely begotten Son of the living God, mankind's only Savior. Second, the glorious Body of that Man is the Church, the Body of Christ. With regard to the former, Paul's six-chaptered Epistle to the Ephesians reveals Jesus to be the Head of the Church, the Temple, the Family, the Body, the Wife, and the Army. Like the ornamented central shaft of the golden lampstand in the tabernacle of Moses, our exalted Head stands tall above all things, having been given executive authority over all that is Heaven and earth as well as the name that is above every name.

Jesus was the Seed planted into the earth in order to produce a supernatural crop—a spiritual family of men and women in His own image and likeness. He died for our sins, was buried, and rose again the third day according to the Scriptures. Jesus then ascended into Heaven, led captivity captive, and gave gifts unto men (Eph. 4:8). From His Davidic throne, our risen King has poured out His Spirit, sending forth His own Spirit into the hearts of men.

The apostle Paul described this Pentecostal experience in Colossians 1:27 as a mystery that had been hidden from ages and generations—"Christ in you, the hope of glory." In the phrase "Christ in *you*," "you" is a plural pronoun. *I* am not Christ. *You* are not Christ. But together, corporately, collectively, *we* comprise the fullness of Him whose present reign is destined to fill all things.

This new corporate creation is further delineated by Paul in Ephesians as the "new man," "the inner man," and "a perfect man" (Eph. 2:15; 3:16; 4:13,24).

Christ is the new nature, the new creation Man.

Christ Is Transcendent

Christ is transcendent, having risen and ascended above all things. *Webster's Dictionary* says that to *transcend* is "to rise above, to surpass; to excel; to be outside the range of; to go beyond the limits of; to be superior to." It adds that *transcendent* means "supreme in excellence; surpassing others; beyond human knowledge; extraordinary." It is derived from the Latin *transcendere*, taken from *trans* ("across") and *scandere* ("to climb").

Jesus is the One who "climbed over" all things, even the mountain called death. Jesus is the Overcomer. We can illustrate by considering the two kinds of vines: those that creep and those that climb (by virtue of their inward nature). The old man is a creepy crawler. Adam is prejudiced, but Jesus died for every creeping thing. The new nature, the Christ nature, is a climber. The word and ministry of reconciliation, a ministry without prejudice, enables the Christian to climb over his own wall instead of climbing all over his brother. As Christians we are called to turn the lion loose upon ourselves and the Lamb upon everybody else.

Jesus Christ is higher than any other, crowned with glory and honor. Our ascended King is the heir of all things. John the Baptist, who understood that His greater Messianic cousin must increase, made this declaration.

Jn. 3:31, NIV

The one who comes from above is above all; the one who comes from the earth [Adam] *belongs to the earth, and speaks* [prejudicially] *as one from the earth. The one who comes from heaven is above all.*

Jesus is the Light of the world; the divine Lamp from Heaven shines above the brightness of the sun. The brightness of the Father's glory, He came to enlighten every nation, and deliver men from the dark tyranny of prejudice and fear. Jesus adds and multiplies. The devil subtracts and divides.

Jesus Himself declared His celestial origin (Jn. 8:23). Earth's rightful King understood that all authority comes from above. The exalted Christ sits enthroned far above all principality, power, might, and dominion. He is the Firstborn among many brethren, made higher than the kings of the earth, higher than the heavens. His ways and thoughts are higher. His name is higher. His anointing is higher. His offering was higher. His wisdom and love are higher (see Is. 55:9; Phil. 2:9; Heb. 1:9; 10:8-10; Jas. 3:17; 1 Pet. 4:8).

This transcendent One humbled Himself, condescending to the low estate of men. In His incarnation, the Word was made flesh and tabernacled among us. Paul declared,

Eph. 4:10, NIV

He who descended is the very one who ascended higher than all heavens, in order to fill the whole universe.

Believers in union with the exalted One have been raised up with Him to share His throne. We are admonished to set our affection on things which are above, not on things on the earth (Col. 3:2). Everything good and perfect flows down from Him who is above. All prejudice is earthy, at enmity with the name and nature of the risen, transcendent Christ.

Christ Is Altogether New

The Bible is divided into the Old and New Testaments. The essence of each shows the difference between our old nature in Adam and our new nature in Christ. This basic difference is described by two words, *law* and *grace*.[2]

True Christians have experienced regeneration, the new birth. The "natural face" of James 1:23 is literally our "genesis face," or the face of our birth. Our "natural face" is the face of the new nature. The Man in the mirror (of the Word) is the new man! The glory of the Old Testament and the old nature was mirrored in the face of Moses. The glory of the New Testament and the new nature is now revealed in the face of Jesus Christ. The law came through Moses, but grace and truth, the key ingredients of our new heart, came through Jesus Christ.

Paul explained in Second Corinthians 3:18 that our growth in grace is "from glory to glory"—out of glory and into glory—out of the glory of the law and into the surpassing glory of grace and truth; out of the dissipating glory of man and into the unfading glory of our Lord; out of the passing and into the permanent. Jesus fulfilled the law and the prophets, consecrating for us a new and living way through His shed blood.

When the Lamb of God died on the cross, the Mosaic veil was rent from the top to the bottom. The law was finished. Grace and truth prevailed. An age, an order, an era, was changed. This happened 2,000 years ago, literally and historically. Our Savior died by violence to fulfill the first covenant; then He rose in triumph to forever establish the New Covenant.

Know this: These same covenantal principles are operative every time God changes an order, whether it is national or personal. These dynamics are an active part of every revival, every fresh outpouring of the Holy Ghost, from early Church history to the present outpouring of God's Spirit. These same truths also apply to the progressive unfolding of the Christ nature in the life of the individual Christian.

When the New Covenant was established, the priesthood was changed from the Levitical economy to the order of Melchisedec, the royal priesthood of Jesus. The law, the Levitical order, was prejudiced and therefore limited. It was weak through the flesh, only ministering to one nation (or "denomi-nation"). The more excellent ministry of the New Testament is unlimited, ministering forgiveness to all men. Jesus' priesthood is altogether new.

Christians have a new nature only because we have been covenantally joined to the Lord! He is the true Vine, and we are the branches. The word the apostle Paul used to describe the "new" creation is *kainos*, which means "new (especially in freshness)." It refers to that which is unaccustomed, unused, or "new" in form or quality, something of a different nature from what has existed previously. In other words, it denotes something completely brand-new!

The other Greek word translated "new" in the King James Version is *neos*. It signifies that which is new with respect to time, that which is recent. But *kainos* has to do with the quality or nature of a thing.

Thayer's Greek Lexicon says that with respect to form, *kainos* means "recently made, fresh, unused, unworn; new, which as recently made is superior to what it succeeds"; with respect to substance, it means "of a new kind, unprecedented, novel, uncommon, unheard of."[3] *Kittel's Theological Dictionary of the New Testament* sums up this principle. As distinct from *neos*, "new in time," it describes *kainos* as "new in nature" (with the implication of "better")![4] The New Testament abounds with things that are altogether new (*kainos*), showing the characteristics of our brand-new, unbiased nature in Christ (see

Mt. 9:17; 13:52; 26:28; Mk. 1:27; 16:17; Jn. 13:34; Eph. 2:15; 4:24; 2 Pet. 3:13; Rev. 2:17; 3:12; 14:3; 21:5).

The covenant of marriage portrays and summarizes this truth. Marriage is not a 50-50 partnership; it is a merger of identities. The resulting union is a wholly new person (two become one). In the same way Christ, the new creation Man, is altogether new.

Christ Is Not Prejudiced—He Is Not Divided

We are all called to speak the same thing, perfectly joined together with the same mind and judgment. Christ is not "divided." This word in First Corinthians 1:13, *merizo*, means "to part, to divide into; to disunite." Jesus' Kingdom is not divided; such dissension brings desolation, which lays waste everything it influences.

The apostle Paul warned of these "divisions" when he wrote to the church at Corinth (1 Cor. 1:10; 11:18; 12:25). He used the word *schisma*, which means "a split or gap" (schism). (Compare this with the verb *schizo*, which means "split or sever.") There are not two natures in the believer—only one. The old man has been crucified. Too many Christians are double-minded spiritual schizophrenics. Remember, Adam is prejudiced, but Christ loves all men.

Paul used a different word for "divisions" in First Corinthians 3:3 to correct the carnality of the saints with regard to their ministerial prejudice. *Dichostsis* means "disunion, dissension," and it could also be rendered as "a standing apart; sedition."

Real Christians have put on the new Man, which is re-newed in knowledge after the image of Him who created all things: "...there is neither Greek nor Jew, circumcision nor uncircumcision, Barbarian, Scythian, bond nor free: but Christ is all, and in all" (Col. 3:11). In this new Spirit-filled life, one's nationality, race, gender, education, or social position is unimportant. Whether a person has Christ is what matters, and He is equally available to all. Again, the only thing that counts with God is becoming a *new creation*.

2 Cor. 5:17, NIV

Therefore, if any one is in Christ, he is a new creation; the old is gone, the new has come!

God is one. We are to keep the unity of the Spirit until we come into the unity of the faith. Unity cannot be created; it can only be kept. All real unity intrinsically flows from the relationship between the Father and the Son, and it is essentially based upon the seven absolutes mentioned by the apostle Paul (Eph. 4:4-6; see also Jn. 17).

The ministry of Jesus and His true Church is a ministry without prejudice. These ten are the major injustices currently hurting and dividing our lives, homes, and ministries:

1. Racial prejudice.
2. Sexual prejudice (gender).
3. Chronological prejudice (age).
4. Geographical prejudice (location).
5. Educational prejudice (how much).
6. Financial prejudice (how much).

7. Physical prejudice (appearance).

8. Denominational prejudice (favorite group).

9. Ministerial prejudice (favorite preacher).

10. Doctrinal prejudice (favorite teaching).

This volume focuses particularly on the first two of these problems. Moreover, there are ten types of relationships through which these ten prejudices can work (causing a myriad of problems). They can build walls within the following relationships:

1. Between an individual and Jesus.

2. Between a local church and Jesus.

3. Between husbands and wives.

4. Between parents and children.

5. Between employers and employees.

6. Between sheep and their shepherds or other sheep.

7. Between shepherds.

8. Between local churches.

9. Between local areas (geographical groups).

10. Between nations.

Everything outside of the Christ nature is a lying vanity. These walls are not real; they exist only in our minds—not His. The mind of Christ, the mind of the Father, is a mind of humility and love, one without walls. Jesus Christ destroyed them all through rending the veil of His own flesh. He rent the veil and broke down the "middle" wall of partition (Mt. 27:51; Eph. 2:14–18). Every wall of prejudice has been built in the middle of man, in the soul that contains his will. The Greek word for wall is *phragmos* and means "a fence, or inclosing barrier." It is akin to *phrasso*, which means "to block up, to silence, to stop." These man-made walls have carried us into captivity and imprisoned God's people.

From man's perspective, these walls are still there, looming insurmountable from the vantage point of the dust of the lower nature. If one changes the spelling of w-a-l-l to w-i-l-l, he can better understand why men fight each other. Prejudiced people will not bend. They will not change their minds. Instead they desire their conscience to be your guide. They scorn repentance and refuse to let go their prejudices, even though these walls are vanities, nothings, idols.

The three great walls addressed in this volume—gender, race, and nationality—are deeply rooted in the pride and conceit of the carnal mind. The Old Testament Israelites refused to enter the land because of unbelief. They used as their excuse the giants and the walled cities. A walled city is an image of the proud, blinded mind. These endtimes are marked by unprecedented spiritual warfare, but we need not fear the giants and their enclosed cities. The Babylonian walls of religion and prejudice are coming down by the Word of the Lord! Note this prophetic progression:

The following Old Testament examples reveal a spiritual sequence. The prophet Daniel saw the handwriting on the wall of religious confusion. The prophet Ezekiel dug through the wall of secret sins. The prophetic army in Joel scaled over the wall of desolation. The prophet David rejoiced and leaped over the wall of old limitations. The prophetic army of Joshua walked together in the same direction for seven days, all shouted with one voice, and the wall of the enemy fell (see Josh. 6:20; Ps. 18:29; Ezek. 8:7-10; Dan. 5:5; Joel 2:7-11)!

There are no walls in His more excellent ministry. Jesus has already destroyed every barrier. Our shout of faith is not to pull the walls down, but to celebrate His victory! The king-priest ministry of Jesus after the order (manner, similitude) of Melchisedec is a ministry without prejudice, without walls.

This introductory chapter has announced His glorious Church to be a supernatural army of living stones, built together to become the habitation of God in the earth. We as believers are a new creation, for Christ is the altogether new nature, the new Man we have received. Christ transcends all prejudice. Above all, in Christ the true Church is not prejudiced or divided. We love and serve all men, having received His commission, the word and ministry of reconciliation.

Acts 17:28, KJV

For in Him we live, and move, and have our being....

Phil. 1:21, KJV

For to me to live is Christ....

Christ is in and among all of us, and His Spirit is not prejudiced! Christ, the Seed of God, is and always has been a *spiritual* seed. The new nature has nothing to do with gender, race, or nationality.

Why are men prejudiced? How are these man-made walls built? Before we discuss the three prejudices, we will begin our examination by demonstrating that they are based on Adam's greatest fear: rejection.

Chapter Two

Man's Greatest Fear: Rejection

"...God is no respecter of persons."

Acts 10:34

In Christ, there is no prejudice of gender, race, or nation. The basic foundation of these three great Adamic walls is man's insecurity, energized by the spirit of fear. Man's greatest fear is that he will not be received, respected, and loved. Tormented by this demon of rejection, man longs for acceptance.

The whole scenario of Acts 10–11 is a lesson about prejudice: God does not show favoritism, but He accepts people from every nation who fear Him. Peter's vision and the unprecedented outpouring of the Holy Spirit upon Cornelius' household teach us that God's heart is toward all humankind.

Prejudice is hate, and hate is learned behavior. A lot of us are like Peter. He had all his preconceived ideas and his formula from Acts 2:38 down pat. But God knew how to shake him up!

Acts 10:11-13, KJV

And saw heaven opened, and a certain vessel descending unto him, as it had been a great sheet knit at the four corners, and let down to the earth:

Wherein were all manner of fourfooted beasts of the earth, and wild beasts, and creeping things, and fowls of the air.

And there came a voice to him, Rise, Peter; kill, and eat.

"Rise, Peter. Kill your prejudice and take unto yourself creeping things!" The Spirit realm opened as Peter beheld a "vessel" descending unto him. This word in Acts 9:11 means "a vessel or implement; a wife as contributing to the usefulness of the husband." The apostle witnessed a picture of the Bride of Christ, the Church. It was knit at the four corners, showing the universality of the Body of Christ. Within were all "manner" (custom or habit) of beasts and "creeping things," representing all kinds of people from every nation.

This is a hard question, but would you lay down your life for a creeping thing? Would you die for a creep? Jesus did. He died for you and me. Peter learned that what God has cleansed or purified by the shed blood of His Son is neither common nor defiled.

Acts 10:34, KJV

Then Peter opened his mouth, and said, Of a truth I perceive that God is no respecter of persons.

Acts 10:34, TLB

Then Peter replied, "I see very clearly that the Jews are not God's only favorites!"

This powerful statement summarizes this entire volume. The phrase "respecter of persons" is translated from the word *prosopoleptes* and means "an accepter of a face (individual), (specifically) one exhibiting partiality." *Prosopoleptes* is taken from two words:

1. *prosopon* = "(the visage); the front (as being towards view), the countenance, aspect, appearance, surface; by implication, presence, person."

2. *lambano* = "to get hold of, seize upon."

To show respect of persons (face) in any form—be it gender, race, or nationality—is ungodliness. God does not embrace one face above another. He is not motivated by or judges according to surface appearances. The will of God for every believer is to be conformed to the image of Jesus Christ, and Jesus did not regard or look at the external qualities of men.

1 Sam. 16:7, KJV

...The Lord seeth not as man seeth; for man looketh on the outward appearance, but the Lord looketh on the heart.

Rom. 2:11, KJV

For there is no respect of persons with God.

In both testaments, it is clear that with God there is no respect of persons (see also Deut. 1:17; 10:17; 16:19; 2 Chron. 19:7; Job 34:19; Ps. 82:1-2; Gal. 2:6; Eph. 6:9; Col. 3:25; Jas. 2:4).

Jn. 3:16, KJV

For God so loved the world, that He gave His only begotten Son…

Accepted in the Beloved

Acts 10:35, KJV

But in every nation he that feareth Him, and worketh righteousness, is accepted with Him.

Man's greatest fear is rejection. It is the evil root of all prejudice. However, in Christ, this dilemma is solved—man is "accepted"! In the Greek this word is *dektos* and means "approved; propitious." Taken from the root *dechomai* ("to receive"), it can also mean "a person or thing who has been regarded favorably."

Through the blood of the Lamb, we have received the forgiveness of sins. Paul announced in Ephesians 1:6 that we have been "made accepted" in the Beloved. The word used here is *chaitoo*, which means "to grace, to endue with special honor." Its root, *charis*, is the Greek word for grace.

Fearing rejection, men and women are ever seeking approval. Because of fleshly insecurities, they continuously perform for one another. In the Church world, this motive is often especially evident among preachers, singers, and musicians. Yet every human performance is also accompanied by an awful thing— a grade.

The battle of the sexes, hatred between the races, strife among the nations (or denominations)— all are manifestations of Adam's inward restlessness. Until an individual is secure in his Christlikeness, there can be no peace.

The teenagers in our homes and the spiritual adolescents in our churches say and do dumb things to get attention. "Look at me!" is their cry. Once they begin to understand that they are already somebody in Christ, "accepted in the beloved" through His finished work, their immature antics will cease.

Fear brings shame and embarrassment. No one seems happy or satisfied with himself. Short people wear platform shoes, and tall people walk around slumped over. Folks with kinky hair want straight hair, while others want their straight hair to be curled. Some blacks want to be white, and white people lay out in the sun all day so that they can become black. In more extreme cases, some men want to be women, while some women want to be men. The answer to all this human frustration is the love of God.

The Samaritan woman in John 4 had been married to five husbands. This is a picture of the Church married to an experience governed by the five natural senses. Still frustrated, this woman was flirting with man number six (the number of man). But when she met the seventh Man, her life was changed. She dropped her waterpot and became a waterpot. She drank from Him; then she ran into the city to herald the good news. Only Jesus can satisfy!

1 Jn. 4:18, KJV

There is no fear in love; but perfect love casteth out fear: because fear hath torment. He that feareth is not made perfect in love.

Perfect love is mature love, void of all prejudices. Only the love of God in Christ Jesus can cast out fear. Fear has "torment" or "penal infliction"(punishment). Jesus is our Jubilee, releasing us from the prison house of anxiety and condemnation. The wonderful fruit of being saved and forgiven is that we can now arise in the love of God and forgive everyone for everything!

The more excellent ministry of our risen, reigning King-Priest is a ministry without condemnation. Notwithstanding, the pain of rejection has fostered a disposition among many of God's people that is most alarming. That pitiful religious attitude says, "I cannot have anything. I cannot do anything. I cannot be anything. And if I can, it won't last!" The Spirit of God despises that kind of "stinkin' thinkin'."

Prov. 17:15, KJV

He that justifieth the wicked, and he that condemneth the just, even they both are abomination to the Lord.

The Hebrew word here for "abomination" means "something disgusting (morally); an abhorrence, especially idolatry or an idol." It comes from a root that means "to loathe, detest." It disgusts Jehovah when men justify their own lawlessness, and it is equally appalling when they commit the abomination of condemnation!

Mankind has been stifled by the spirit of fear. To compensate for their insecurities and instabilities, men try to make a small man tall by cutting off the legs of the tall man. Men and women put each other down. Races and nationalities constantly compare themselves among themselves, which is not wise.

Stop condemning the just! Stop bad-mouthing the redeemed! Stop putting down yourself and others whom Jesus has washed in His blood and justified by His grace. Don't justify the lawlessness of the beast nature; neither rail against the righteousness of God and His new creation. Jesus never condemned the just. Jesus never condemned anyone. Our words must become constructive, not destructive. We must be delivered from our prejudices. This is not a day to tear down, but to build up.[1]

The Man in the Mirror

Paul declared in Second Corinthians 4:4 that Christ is the "image of God." *Antichrist* is any other image, an idol, something "instead of Christ." It is my fervent prayer that you become aware of the presence of the greater One who lives in your heart. May you receive a progressive vision of Him:

1. As He is, the exalted One.

2. As He is in you, the greater One.

3. As He is through you, the ministering One.

This first principle speaks of our worship. The second speaks of our warfare in the heavenlies; and the third, of our welfare to others as we release Christ from within. In these days of global revival, Christ is not coming down;

He is coming up and out! No longer a garden enclosed (by our previous prejudices), we can now allow the spices of His grace and truth to spread to a hurting world.

The point is that there are two images of you: Christ, (which is His image of you) and antichrist (which is your image of you). The images we have of ourselves (male-female, black-white, Jew-Greek) are the ones we tend to believe instead of the One who is real— Christ, the Man in the mirror.

Two images create duality, and duality is idolatry. God hates mixture. To be "double minded," as referred to in James 1:8 (KJV), is to be, literally, "double-souled." Weymouth's translation says that such a one is "a man of two minds, undecided in every step he takes." The Amplified Bible adds that he is "hesitating, dubious, ir-resolute...unstable and unreliable and uncertain about everything he thinks, feels, decides." This kind of mind is the prejudiced mind, focused on God *and* gender, or race, or nationality!

James 1:16-18 further illumines the nature of God, the Christ nature. We are the sons of light, and God is Father. The Father is not double-minded, and neither is His seed. The word for "kind" in James 1:18 is *tis* and it means "a certain kind," a Kingdom species, if you will. Note as well that we have been birthed by the word of truth.

Jas. 1:23-24, KJV

> *For if any be a hearer of the word, and not a doer, he is like unto a man beholding his natural face in a glass:*
>
> *For he beholdeth himself, and goeth his way, and straightway forgetteth what manner of man he was.*

The word for "beholding" in James 1:23 means to "contemplate or gaze upon." What are we looking at? Our "natural face." Who is this Man in the glass? Who is the Man in the mirror? As with the laver in the Mosaic Tabernacle, we understand the mirror to represent the Word of God.

The word describing the "natural" face of the man is *genesis* and means "nativity, nature." The literal rendering of this phrase in James 1:23 is "the face of his birth"! What birth does it refer to? The one in verse 18! The Man in the mirror is the *new Man*. He is neither male nor female, black nor white, Jew nor Greek. And this new man has but a single eye (Mt. 6:22-24; 2 Cor. 11:3; Heb. 12:2). We gaze into the Word of God to behold, not Adam's sinfulness, but the simplicity of Christ's righteousness! We behold our "natural" face—the face of a new heart received by new birth—His nature.

In the "glass" of God's Word, we behold the glory of the Lord. And where is this glory revealed? Second Corinthians 3:18–4:6 says that this glory is revealed in the face of Jesus Christ. The Man in the mirror is the new Man, mirroring His face. Our gaze is not focused upon human weakness, fear, sorrow, or limitation, nor is it focused on our gender, race, or nationality. Rather we look unto Jesus, unto His strength, His faith, His joy, and His ministry!

Keep gazing and contemplating, child of God. You are becoming like the Man in the mirror, becoming like the One you worship. You are being changed, transfigured, transformed into that same image—His image, His face.

The first of the Ten Commandments warns against false images. The Hebrew margin of Exodus 20:3 reads, "Thou shalt have no other gods before My face!" Many cannot see the glory of the Lord revealed in the face of Jesus Christ. Their limited understanding is fastened upon darkness, disease, death, and damnation. Their focus is male or female, black or white, Jew or Greek. What has blinded them? Their face is in the way of His face. Man's image of himself stands between him and God's image for man. This is like a veil that must be rent, an alabaster box that must be broken, a wall of Jericho that must be shouted down!

Consider this important thought: *Sin is a mistaken identity!* Prejudice abounds because men do not know who they are. They ignorantly worship antichrist instead of Christ.

Hamartiology is that branch of theology that deals with the doctrine of sin. It is so named because of *hamartia*, the Greek word for "sin." This word is akin to the verb *hamartano*, which means "to miss the mark (and so not share in the prize)." The Hebrew word *chata* is comparable; it means "to miss." Sin means to "miss the mark." One of the Greek words for "mark" is *charagma*, hence the English word *character*. To fall short of the mark is to fall short of the character of Christ— sin is a mistaken identity!

Here lies the crux of the matter, the recurring theme of this entire volume. From God's perspective, our identity is not measured or determined by gender, race, or nationality. Our identity as the new creation is completely defined "in Christ." He is the sum total of our existence.

When men get their attention (the focus of their marriage, their job, their ministry) on the issues of male or female, black or white, and Jew or Greek, they look away from Christ and miss His character and love. They *sin*, and come short of the glory that He longs to share with them all.

Man's greatest fear is rejection, the root of all prejudice. But faith, the opposite of fear, is the seedbed of hope. Christ is in and among us all, and Christ is not prejudiced! Christ, the Seed of God, is and always has been a *spiritual* seed. The new nature has nothing to do with gender, race, or nationality.

As this Joshua generation goes forth to possess the land and fulfill the Great Commission, we must put the fear of rejection under our feet. And the first giant we must confront is prejudice based upon gender— the battle of the sexes.

Part Two

Gender

"...neither male nor female...."

Galatians 3:28

Foreword by Dr. Fuchsia Pickett

It is difficult to estimate the damage that has been done to the Body of Christ because of prejudice against gender. What giftings, ministries, consolations, and virtues have been inadvertantly robbed from the Church because of strong prejudicial discrimination against the female gender. And what overt harm has been perpetrated on the Church because of women's harsh reactions against the limitations placed upon them that frustrated their expression of the giftings of God in their lives. In each case, the lack of understanding of our priority as believers—to become Christlike in character and in deed—has kept the Church from coming into the maturity and oneness that God intends for her to demonstrate.

As a young mother barely 20 years of age, God called me to preach and teach His Word. Although I had never heard of a woman preacher, I did not think I had an option to disobey the audible voice of God to me when He sovereignly visited me. He opened doors for my training, anointed me to preach His Word, and then opened doors for the ministry He had called me to fulfill. In almost 50 years of ministry, I have never lacked a place to minister the Word and to teach the Scriptures as He called me to do. And because many men and women have testified to their lives being changed through the messages they heard, I did not feel the need to consult with a committee or board to see if their theology or prejudice agreed with the calling of God on my life. Yet I certainly have been accountable to several different denominations and fellowships of ministers, and have enjoyed wide acceptance from them.

Nevertheless, I am grateful for this scholarly and sensitive work that Pastor Varner is presenting to the Body of Christ, for it will surely be helpful to the sincere believer, man or woman, who has questions regarding God's eternal purposes for mankind. We have labored so futilely under "fallen doctrine" of man's supremacy, taken from the Genesis account, that declares that man shall rule over the woman, accepting that as divine order instead of the result of the fall as it is in reality. Redemption is intended to restore man and woman to God's original intent for them.

Restoration, by definition, means that what is being restored will become more perfect in beauty than its original design. Before the fall, Adam and his wife, though free from prejudice, were not mature in the character of God. Character is a result of our choices, and as we know, Adam and Eve failed in that regard. God's character will be manifest in the men and women of God who choose to be cleansed from gender prejudice and to allow the Spirit of Christ to rule them. They will be restored to the freedom from prejudice Adam and Eve enjoyed, and will also demonstrate the character of God that the first couple did not attain to. They will walk together in unity of purpose and expression as God intended for them from the beginning.

It is time for the Church to come into her inheritance, growing up into the Head in all things, and putting away the fallen doctrine of mankind that has so thwarted the purposes of God in the earth. A careful reading of this book by sincere believers who are willing to experience a divine paradigm shift, to accept the truths of God's Word regarding man and woman, will do much to bring healing and restoration to the Body of Christ today.

Chapter Three

Womanhood From God's Perspective

"...she shall be called Woman...."

Genesis 2:23

Christ is not prejudiced. His nature transcends every human bias. He is not a sexist. He is neither male nor female.

Prejudice of gender is the first of three great prejudices because it is at the root of most other bigotry. In my opinion, it is often the biggest wall of all.

Men are afraid of women. Women are afraid to be women. Great male preachers won't let females preach, dismissing them to the prayer room or nursery. At the same time these men unabashedly refer to themselves as the Bride of Christ! To have respect of persons or to show partiality is sin. Earthy ignorance has little to do with the wisdom that is from above.

The primary cause of male-female prejudice is insecurity, and the root of this weakness is the spirit of fear.

Men and women are paranoid because they are un-schooled in the Word of God. The Scriptures reveal the unique, divinely ordained roles of each gender. Outside of the knowledge of these truths, a great wall exists.

Chapters One and Two established that Christ, the new nature, transcends these sexual differences. Adam, whether male or female man, is the one who is biased.

Gal. 3:28, KJV

There is neither Jew nor Greek, there is neither bond nor free, there is neither male nor female: for ye are all one in Christ Jesus.

Jesus' cross and the blood of the New Covenant canceled the old order, the shadow of greater things to come. In the Kingdom of God there are no hierarchies, no second-class citizenships, and no spiritual stepchildren. Each person is an unrivaled redeemed individual and a joint-heir with Christ—regardless of sex, race, nationality, or position in society. But centuries of tradition aren't easily changed.

Christian women are weary of their plight of being assigned a second-class status. Forbidden to participate in most positions of church leadership, many have pursued other avenues of expression. Florence Nightingale said that she would have given the church her head, her hands, and her heart, but the church would not have them. She was told to go back and crochet in her mother's drawing room.[1] Women cry out, but there are not enough words to describe the thwarting opposition. They long for understanding, but doors still piously close. Even those illusive opportunities that seem to be open doors have residual, restrictive superstitions rusting in their hinges.

Did God intend for women to have a secondary place in the Church, or do they have full personhood?

In the Beginning

In the beginning, the only thing that was "not good" was man's aloneness; the woman was fashioned to be man's help meet. God's creation was not complete without woman. The first chapter of Genesis states God's original intent and purpose in creating man both male and female. The second chapter shows how He did it. Woman wasn't an afterthought, but a vital part of God's original plan:

Gen. 1:26-28, KJV

*And God said, Let Us make man in Our image, after Our likeness: and let **them** have dominion....*

*So God created man in His own image, in the image of God created He him; male and female created He **them**.*

*And God blessed **them**, and God said unto **them**, Be fruitful, and multiply, and replenish the earth, and subdue it....*

God's initial mandate for humankind (man and woman) was to fill the earth and rule over it. Any supremacy was swallowed up in unity. God's command was given to "them," not "him."

God's earliest blueprint must govern our thinking with regard to gender. *Ha 'adam*, with the definite article *ha*, used in Genesis 1 for "man," is not the proper name Adam with an article. *Ha 'adam* is a generic term meaning "humanity" or "mankind." Genesis 5:1-2 states God blessed Adam and Eve and called their name Man (*ha 'adam*) in the day they were created. After this, the article is dropped and *'Adam* becomes the proper name of the man Adam. God did not give His command to rule to just one person, but to all humanity, including the soon-to-be-made woman!

Genesis 2:18 says that Eve was Adam's "help meet." The woman was created to help, surround, protect, and aid the man. The word "meet" indicates that she was to be in the presence of the man, fronting or facing him, being his corresponding counterpart and appropriate mate— they would answer to each other. The Septuagint (the Greek Old Testament) translates "help meet" with the word *homoios*, which means "of the same nature, like, or similar," and signifies equal force or rank. Various Bible translations reveal Eve to be Adam's own species and kind, a counterpart, a helper suitably equal—intellectually, morally, and physically fit—for matching him.

"Help" is a word frequently used in reference to the Lord Himself, especially in the Book of Psalms (see Ps. 10:14; 22:11; 28:7; 46:1; 54:4; 72:12; 86:17; 119:173,175; 121:1-2). Therefore it is not a degrading position for the woman. Fifteen times it is used to mean "superior strength." Its verb form indicates aid or supply that the individual cannot provide for himself— the woman is the "help meet" for the man. Woman wasn't created just as man's assistant or server. She was to be his associate, a co-worker with full rights and privileges. She was added strength to fill his weaknesses.

Men argue for the subordination of women based upon the creative order. They say that the woman was created *after* the man, and is therefore secondary to him. With that same logic, we observe that animals and dirt were created *before* Adam, yet are not superior to him! God was more concerned about His commission to Adam (male and female) than He was about the order in which they were created and formed.

Eve completed Adam; she was derived but not inferior. She was not created to serve Adam, but to serve with Adam. As a woman works and rules, she does not lose her femininity but rather regains it.

In Eden, there was no job assignment according to gender. Man and woman had the same destiny and a shared humanity. In First Peter 3:7, the apostle did not say that the wife is the "weaker vessel," but that her husband is to treat her "as" the weaker vessel. The devil walks about "as" a roaring lion, but he isn't one. The apostle was teaching each husband to defer to his wife, to be gentle and kind, to have knowledge of her, to maintain an awareness of how to relate to her. Together, husband and wife are joint-heirs of the grace of life!

Genesis 2:21 says that Eve was taken from Adam's side, but the woman was not created just to be man's sidekick! The word "rib" is a mistranslation and should read "side" or "chamber." The Greek word for this in the Septuagint is *pleura*. It is used to describe our Lord's "side" from which the wife of the last Adam was taken (Jn. 19:34; 20:20-27; see also 1 Cor. 15:45)!

Eve was called "Woman" or *Isha*, the feminine form of *ish*, which means "a notable man of high degree." This noblewoman was man with a womb. But Eve, the mother of all living, furnishes a bigger picture. She points to the Bride of both testaments.

Israel, Jehovah's Old Testament wife and a type of the Church, is often referred to as a woman. This is seen in:

1. The Book of Psalms (Ps. 9:14; 45:13).

2. The Book of Isaiah (see Is. 1:8; 10:32; 16:1; 22:4; 37:22; 52:2; 54:5; 62:4-5,11).

3. The Book of Jeremiah (see Jer. 3:6-8,14,20; 4:11,31; 6:2,14,23,26; 8:11,19-22; 9:1,7; 14:17; 31:22; 49:4).

4. The Book of Lamentations (see Lam. 1:6,15; 2:1-22; 3:48; 4:3,10,22).

5. The Minor Prophets (see Hos. 2:19-20; Mic. 1:13; 4:8-13; Zeph. 3:14; Zech. 9:9).

This pattern is continued in the New Testament with the Church, the Bride of Christ (see Jn. 3:29; Rom. 7:2-4; 2 Cor. 11:2-3; Eph. 5:22-33; Col. 1:18,24; Rev. 12:1-5; 21:2,9; 22:17).

One renowned commentator of Scripture wrote, "If man is the head, she [woman] is the crown, a crown to her husband, the crown of the visible creation... The woman was made of a rib out of the side of Adam; not made out of his head to rule over him, nor out of his feet to be trampled upon by him, but out of his side to be equal with him, under his arm to be protected, and near his heart to be beloved."[2]

Gen. 2:18, KJV

And the Lord God said, It is not good that the man should be alone....

This verse is void of any aspect of man's authority over woman. Its immediate context is reproduction, not masculine preeminence! Had God created woman first He would have created man for the same reason: Neither can reproduce alone. Paul summed this up, ruling out any primal position of the man over the woman:

1 Cor. 11:11-12, KJV

Nevertheless neither is the man without the woman, neither the woman without the man, in the Lord.

For as the woman is of the man, even so is the man also by the woman; but all things of God.

Without this revelation, Paul's other statements in that same chapter remain unbalanced.

Historically, Israel was different from the other Oriental nations with regard to their God and their treatment of each other. Women in Israel enjoyed a station not generally experienced in the East. The Jews, holding to the revelation given to Moses of woman's endowments, worth, and rightful position, kept the woman in high esteem and affection. The Levitical law protected the weakness of the woman, preserved her freedom, and promoted her rights.

Compared with her heathen neighbors, the Old Testament woman had greater liberties, more varied tasks, more important work, and a more respected position. Sadly, the evolution of Jewish religious tradition replaced the Mosaic model. But real New Testament Christianity restored full emancipation to womanhood. Wherever Jesus Christ is preached and obeyed, the woman is esteemed as man's beloved companion and confidante, a joint-heir of grace and truth.

To reiterate, the Book of Genesis is the seed-plot of all biblical revelation. When God planned to create mankind, He made "them" in His own image and likeness and gave "them" dominion. He commissioned "them" to multiply, replenish the earth, and subdue it. They ruled together as one. This was God's initial intention toward women— she was to have dominion with her husband.

As noted, *ha 'adam* initially was a collective term for mankind, and includes women. Man (mankind) is male and female. Thus, a man and a woman in right relation reveal the image of God, and God is love. Both the mother's love (female) and father's love (male) are necessary to fully express God's divine nature. A mother's love is unconditional love, while father's love is a firm, earned respect. The husband and wife represent the totality of God to their children— the man with his logic, the woman with her compassion; the man with his reasoning, the woman with her intuition. Together, they show their children a complete picture of God's attributes and grace— an unbeatable team.

To properly grasp the root causes for prejudice based on gender, it is essential to understand that the opening chapters of Genesis reveal that the principle of authority and submission was not part of God's original creation. It came later, after the fall, under the curse!

The decade of the 1970s was marked by an accelerated awareness of theocratic government throughout the Body of Christ. Divine order, local church government and structure, authority and submission— these truths that emerged were much needed in the Charismatic community birthed in the 60s. However, the so-called "discipleship controversy" arose because the principle of authority and submission was misunderstood. Consequently, it was carried too far in three key arenas: the *domestic*, husbands taking too much authority over their wives; the *ecclesiastical*, shepherds (pastors) taking too much authority over the sheep (saints); and *translocal*, apostles taking too much authority over local shepherds (elders). These excesses and eventual abuses occurred because men did not fully comprehend the Scriptures.

The Jewish Talmud (not a translation of the Scripture, but a compilation of Jewish tradition) placed "ten curses" upon Eve. But nowhere does the Bible say that God cursed either the man or the woman! Genesis 3:14-17 says that the serpent and the ground were cursed. Adam and Eve were told the consequences of their sin: death.

The blight of sin brought submission, authority, rulership, and oppression into the earth. In Genesis 3:16 the woman was told that there would be a multiplication of her "sorrow and conception" The word "sorrow" means "worrisomeness" and is used to describe Adam's similar predicament in the very next verse. The word "conception" is rendered as "sighing" or "groaning" in the Septuagint, a rendering with which many ancient authorities agree.

The biblical doctrine of authority and submission is not God's ultimate intention for His people. It is a means to an end, not the end itself. Again, this temporary principle operates under the curse. It was not until *after* the transgression that Adam would "rule," have dominion over and govern Eve, or that the woman's "desire" would be to her husband— she was to "stretch out after" or "run after" him. An examination of the etymology of this word also indicates that Eve would "turn away" to her husband. God said to Eve, "You are turning away from Me to your husband, and he will [future tense] rule over you." Ever since Adam fell, his male progeny has sought to subjugate the woman. These conditions were the aftermath of sin, the result of the fall, not the primitive creative design.

Prior to their transgression, the man and the woman were *one*. There was no need for authority or submission; it was swallowed up in the simplicity of their union! To the extent that grace works in the heart of the male, he loses the love of any preeminence or the desire to rule over his wife.

Before the fall, the authoritarian man and submissive woman aren't visible. The frustrated woman withstanding man's bullish aggressiveness came *after* sin and death had gained control of mankind. Before the fall, none of this existed. There is not a single Scripture that indicates it was there.

There is something greater than obedience. The operation of authority and submission necessitates *two* wills—one must come under and submit to the other. Thus, obedience is not the ultimate order of things. The highest order of anything is to *become* it! God wants more than our obedience. He desires us to become one with His will...His *one* will.

Jesus Christ was the pattern for this. In His incarnation He descended from the realm of perfect order and worship into this lower realm of chaos and death (the realm of that which is transient or passing away), that He might deliver men from it. Jesus identified with broken and sinful humanity by lowering Himself into a relationship of authority and submission to the Father. Before His incarnation, He and the Father were *one*. Jesus humbled Himself even further and submitted to Joseph and Mary, and to the law.

Some may suppose these thoughts to belittle the truth of authority and submission; to the contrary, they put this vital principle in its proper perspective. Spiritual authority is the only biblical truth that will experientially bring us out from under the curse! By this primary principle Jesus Christ in His sonship walked out from under bondage and futility, bringing us up and out with Him! We were in His spiritual loins! The fivefold ministry is the only tool Jesus left in the earth to mature His Church. There will be leaders in the local church and divine order in the home "until..." (Eph. 4:11-13).

Again, men tend to deem spiritual authority as all-important or not important at all. The truth is in the middle. The first extreme kills people with legalism, the law of sin and death. The other extreme destroys folks with license. Historically, the legalism of classical Pentecostalism gave way to the rampant license of the Charismatic renewal; but God is bringing both back into balance. In the former, too many preachers were mighty tough on the women. In the latter, some of the women ran to and fro with no regard for divine order, without being accountable either to their husbands or to local church eldership.

Paul dealt with these polarized views in his Epistle to the Galatians, warning the legalistic Judaizers and the fleshly Antinomians. The law kills, spiritually, mentally, and physically. But license kills quicker. Both law and lust abort the divine Seed. When a baby is born, his bones are soft. The structure is there, but it's flexible. The most important thing is that the baby is alive. Therefore the life of the risen Christ in our homes and churches takes precedence over our order or particular style of government.

God's ultimate intention is for man and woman to be *one* within the rent veil, within the Most Holy Place, the place of Jesus' finished work. When the will of the man is one with the will of his God, and the will of the woman is one with the will of her God, their name or nature becomes one. Authority and submission is then swallowed up in singleness and union—the will of the man and the woman harmonize in complete agreement with the Lord. Two become one in the purest and fullest sense of the word.

"They shall be *one* flesh" (Gen. 2:24; compare Deut. 6:4). The word for "one" is *'echad* and means "united." This is a compound unity rather than a single entity. It takes more than one thing to make an *'echad*— a united togetherness. The word for single or solitary is *yachiyd*. Adam was *yachiyd*. Eve was *yachiyd*, but God joined them together to become an *'echad*! Paul quoted this verse in Ephesians 5:31 to describe the relationship between Christ and His Church.

Finally, that the man is said to be the "head" of the woman does not mean that he is the only priest in the home. Such teaching denies the woman personal access to God as well as personal responsibility for her own actions because the husband can nullify her decisions. The Greek word for "head" is *kephale*; and unlike its Hebrew and English counterparts, it does not communicate the meaning of "chief" or "boss." The real Head of the home is Jesus. Two verses are key to this principle:

1 Cor. 11:3, KJV

> *But I would have you know, that the head of every man* [*andros* or "mankind, male and female"] *is Christ; and the* **head** *of the woman is the man* [*aner* or "husband"]; *and the head of Christ is God.*

Eph. 5:23, KJV

> *For the husband is the* **head** *of the wife....*

Any orthodox theologian will contend that there is within the Godhead mutual submission, authority, unity, and oneness beyond human comprehension. So it is covenantally between the man and the woman!

Kephale has never meant decision-maker, superior rank, or final authority. In Paul's day, it was a Gnostic buzzword. Greeks were always looking for the origin of things. The "head" was the *source*. Paul was addressing Greek Christians who were converts from Greek religions. If the apostle had wanted to convey the idea of leader or ruler, he would have used a different Greek word. The Romans and the Greeks who would be reading Paul's Epistles knew that *kephale* meant "source." Eve was derived from Adam— taken from his side. As noted, before the fall, she was not submitted to him; they were one.

True headship in the home and local church is horizontal, not vertical. Jesus is *over* His enemies, but He goes *before* His sheep. This is also true with the concept of true apostleship, those who are to be examples to the flock. Genuine headship demonstrates and focuses upon serving *among* men rather than ruling *over* them. This posture of biblical headship, not lording over others, is the one that men should take with regard to women. Real headship is proven and earned.

Another parallel issue regarding headship and gender prejudice is Paul's instruction in First Corinthians 11:1-17 about the head covering. Suffice it to say, the apostle was more interested in the men removing their head coverings (exampled by the Jewish *tallith*, a sign of reverence before God and of condemnation for sin) than he was in the women wearing one. The intent of that passage is to reveal that Jesus Christ rent the veil so that men and women wouldn't have to wear one on their head or have one on their hearts. Now both men and women can worship God with an unveiled face. For those who want to argue for or against a head covering, Paul concludes:

1 Cor. 11:16, KJV

But if any man seem to be contentious, we have no such custom, neither the churches of God.

The King's Daughter Is All Glorious Within

Deep in the hearts of many women, strong resentments have risen over being limited to the ministry of helps by men who have misinterpreted certain Scriptures. Some have overreacted to this religious male tradition by becoming over-assertive and domineering in order to prove that they do indeed have a ministry. Women who have been put down by men often answer with a wrong motive and spirit. Many want to go forth and "do" something for God. But the secret of all ministry has to do with who you *are* and what you can *be*, not what you can do.

Psalm 45:13-15 describes the king's daughters, those honorable women who have named Jesus Christ as Lord. The Christian woman is to be all glorious within, clothed in gold, a partaker of His own divine nature. God wants to do a work of the Spirit *in* His daughters before He does a work *through* them. The ins and outs of daily living, serving in the home and the local church, is the tapestry of His sustaining grace. Her friends and companions will take notice and follow her. She will quickly become a woman of influence. God will weave the circumstances of a woman's life to work His image into her. Women who truly love King Jesus understand that He alone can usher them into the place of public ministry. Just as a man's ministry gift makes room for him and leads him into greatness, the daughters of Zion will be brought into the king's palace.

In Matthew's Gospel, when Mary poured out the alabaster ointment upon the head of her Lord she ministered to the *head* first. Lady, learn to become a worshiper. The King will begin to share the intimate burdens of His own heart, releasing through you a fragrance of His resurrection life that will inspire everyone you meet. The more you love the Lord, the more you will love your husband, children, and neighbors.

Jesus desires this inward adorning and beauty of the hidden person of the heart. He is after the incorruptible and unfading charm of a gentle and peaceful spirit, one that is not anxious or wrought up and very precious in the sight of God. A woman (or a man) who is meek is courteous, teachable, and open to correction.

The Pentecostal experience of the Holy Ghost Baptism has incorporated women into His Body, giving each of them a part in the manifestation of the Spirit given to edify the whole Body. That same anointing will first deal with one's nature and motives. Is your spirit right? Are your heart and mind receptive and responsive? Have you ministered to the King first?

The Virtuous Woman

Any born-again believer, filled with the Holy Spirit, submitted to the teaching of Jesus Christ, and flowing in the balance of God's Word, is qualified to minister the gospel. Throughout the Word of God it is clear that any such person—whether male or female—has total liberty to fulfill the ministry role to which God has called him or her. The scope of women's ministry throughout the

Scriptures must be underscored by an understanding of the proper attitude toward that ministry.

True submission is mutual and reciprocal: Men and women are to honor each other. In his day Paul commanded that men submit to those who labored with him, and many of these co-laborers were women (Rom. 16:16)! In many cultures and religious denominations, women are treated as servants or slaves. For those who point out that Sarah obeyed Abraham and called him "lord," or "sir," we must also note that God told Abraham, "In all that Sarah hath said unto thee, hearken unto her voice..." (Gen. 21:12; see also 1 Pet. 3:6)! How does Jesus Christ, the Head of the Church, treat *His* Wife? He responds to her with love, patience, compassion, and forgiveness, always seeking to encourage her. Paul's words in Ephesians 5:25-32 reveal His love to be sacrificial, purifying, caring, and unbreakable.

Women's ministry has a vast scope. At the top of the list is the Spirit-filled wife and mother— the virtuous woman— one who is morally righteous, industrious, and God-fearing. Jewish tradition made the mother responsible for teaching and training her son until the age of seven (the most formative years of his life). He would then be turned over to his father.

Though some women are called to active, public ministry, each woman's first responsibility is to her husband and children. The hardest place to be really spiritual is in the home. A woman who cannot demonstrate her ministry in the domestic arena cannot prove it anywhere else. Paul laid the same requirement upon the brethren in ministry (1 Tim. 3:4-5,11-12; see also Lk. 12:26).

The translators of the Septuagint used the word *dunamis* (which means "powerful, able") for "virtuous" when describing Ruth, the determined wife of Boaz (Ruth 3:11). The Hebrew word means "a force" and underscores her strength. The dynamic Holy Ghost woman is a crown to her husband; she is wise, to build her home and family; she is good, bringing the favor of the Lord; and she is a gift from the Lord (see Prov. 12:4; 14:1; 18:22; 19:10).

The "virtuous woman" is thoroughly described in Proverbs 31:10-31. Each of those 22 verses provides a singular revelation of her life and ministry and also furnishes a panoramic picture of the end-time Church, the Wife of Christ. This powerful woman is:

1. Rare, priced far above rubies.

2. Trustworthy.

3. A constant blessing to her husband.

4. Not lazy, and her house is not dirty.

5. Thrifty with her husband's money.

6. A good administrator who works well with others.

7. One who considers things of worth.

8. Strong in character.

9. One who knows that she has done well.

10. Ever industrious.

11. Kind and generous to her neighbors.

12. Not afraid, prepared for the coming storm.

13. Feminine in her dress and demeanor.

14. Noteworthy, for her husband is a leader.

15. One who uses her spare time profitably.

16. One who laughs and is not fearful of the future.

17. One who will not gossip.

18. A careful watcher over her household.

19. Blessed by her husband and children.

20. One with a ministry of excellence.

21. One who fears and worships the Lord.

22. One whose fruit remains.

Simply stated, the "virtuous woman" is trustworthy and hard-working, a woman of thrift, strong in heart, showing great love, with gracious, godly speech— a real spiritual woman who loves Jesus!

Having established that the ministry of women (and men) begins in the home and that all avenues of Kingdom service are blessed in the light of being proven in that primary arena, we now turn to examine the scope of women's public ministry in the Bible, beginning with the Old Testament.

Chapter Four

The Public Ministry of Women in the Bible

"And God blessed them...."

Genesis 1:28

The great wall of partition formed by prejudice between men and women has evolved over the centuries. Ignorance of the Bible and human arrogance among the brethren have caused many to use the Scriptures to hinder and spiritually cripple their sisters in Christ. This and the next chapter take a fresh look at the internal evidence of the Old and New Testaments concerning the public ministry of women and the record of Church history from the time of the Anti-Nicene Church to the present.

Women's ministry in the Bible is a varied one of witness, worth, and wealth, unlimited by age (of person or era), status (situation), heritage, or precedent. Woman has not always been ranked under man, as exampled by the judge Deborah. Woman has often coupled with a man, as was Priscilla with Aquila, in the service of God. Women of the Bible were also used in the ministry of hospitality, as exampled by Mary, Martha, and Lydia. They had great responsibility, such as Phebe, who delivered Paul's great doctrinal Epistle to the saints at Rome.

The life stories of great women fill the pages of the Old Testament, beginning with Eve and her joint lordship with Adam over the earth. Eve was co-regent with her husband, ruling with him as a fully equal partner, sharing dominion with him (Gen. 1:26-28).

Adah was the woman who gave the world its first musician, Jubal (Gen. 4:19-23).

Sarah, wife to the patriarch Abraham, became the mother of nations, the matriarch of all those who walk and live by faith. She typifies the New Testament free-woman, the Church, the heavenly Jerusalem (Gen. 12–22; Gal. 4:21-31). God breathed His Spirit, the "h" sound of *Jah*, into the life of Sarai (which means "dominative"), changing her name, or nature, to Sarah (which means "a female noble; lady, princess, queen").

Rebekah was led and brought by the steward Eliezer to become the bride of Isaac (Gen. 24).

Beautiful Rachel was the mother of Benjamin and the great statesman Joseph (Gen. 29–31).

Jochebed was the woman whose children, Moses, Aaron, and Miriam, became great leaders (Ex. 1–2).

Miriam was a prophetess who led the women of Israel. She was used of God along with Moses and Aaron to redeem and lead His great nation from the house of bondage (Ex. 15:20-21; Mic. 6:4).

The five daughters of Zelophahed asked for and received equal inheritance with the sons of Israel (Num. 27:1-8).

Rahab of Jericho was saved to become the wife of Salmon and the mother of wealthy Boaz. She is mentioned in the faith hall of fame and by the apostle James (see Josh. 2; 6:17-25; Heb. 11:31; Jas. 2:25).

Achsah, the woman who wanted the greater blessing of the upper springs, later became the wife of the judge Othniel (Josh. 15:16-17).

Deborah was a great prophetess who judged Israel for 40 years (Judg. 4–5). Her name means "bee," denoting order and intelligence. This military leader was the only judge to carry the title of a prophet before Samuel. The courageous damsel Jael was her assistant in the destruction of the heathen general Sisera.

Ruth was providentially brought from the land of Moab to become the wife of Boaz. She was the great-grandmother of King David and an ancestress of the Messiah, the Lord Jesus Christ (Ruth 1–4).

Hannah taught her son Samuel to worship God as a child. He grew into the manchild and faithful priest who restored Israel's greatness and later anointed King Saul and King David (1 Sam. 1–3).

Abigail was the woman with beauty and brains who became David's queen (1 Sam. 25; 2 Sam. 3:3).

Huldah was a great prophetess who could interpret and authenticate the Word of God, sparking King Josiah's great national revival that restored true worship to Israel (2 Kings 22:14-20; 2 Chron. 34:22-33).

Noadiah was a false prophetess (a counterfeit of genuine ministry) in the days of Nehemiah (Neh. 6:14; compare Ezek. 13:17).

Esther (Hadassah) became the Queen of Persia and saved the Jewish nation from extermination (Esther 1–10).

Moreover, there are feminine Hebrew pronouns that provide some interesting insights into certain passages. The psalmist mentions a great company of "women" who would publish the Word, and Isaiah addressed the "inhabitress" of Zion and the "woman" who would bring good tidings (Ps. 68:11; Is. 12:6; 40:9).

The Book of Ecclesiastes takes its name from the Greek word *ekklesiastes*, meaning "convener of an assembly." This has also been translated as "leader of a convocation, speaker before the congregation." The book is often referred to by its Hebrew name, *qoheleth*, which is in the *feminine* gender and means "a (female) assembler (lecturer); abstractly, preaching."

Finally, the prophet Joel uttered his famous prophecy concerning the coming of the New Covenant when the Holy Spirit would be poured out without prejudice upon God's sons and daughters, His servants and handmaids (Joel 2:28-32).

Though these examples have been taken from the Old Covenant, the New Testament Scriptures clearly add that they were written for our admonition and learning (Rom. 15:4; 1 Cor. 10:11; see also Acts 3:24; 26:22).

The Old Testament evidence is powerfully conclusive. There is no difference between a man and a woman when ministering the Word of God by the power of His Spirit. It's the same Holy Ghost with a different flavor.

The Public Ministry of Women in the New Testament

With regard to the New Covenant, the primary bottom-line question is, "What was Jesus' attitude toward women?"

The King recognized His daughters' personal worth and their hunger for the Word of God. He restored truth to marriage. He healed women and showed them mercy. Jesus met females without fear and addressed their singular identity. In John 4, He talked publicly with the Samaritan woman, who was considered a nothing by pious Jewish males. He defended widows and used the sacrificial giving of a widow's mite to illustrate the principle of true giving. Jesus touched "unclean" women and allowed women to minister to Him.

Jesus constantly overrode the rabbinical laws to proclaim the truth. He had female disciples. At the worst moment of His life (the cross), all His disciples left Him and fled; that is, all except the women. These same women became the first witnesses of His resurrection. Jesus later rebuked His male apostles for not believing their testimony!

Jesus restored dignity and honor to women. Women were the first messengers of His resurrection. Nowhere in any of the Gospels does our King in any way suppress or put down the opportunity for women to minister to Him or publicly tell others about Him. Note these examples:

Elizabeth prophesied and Mary's Magnificat was the prophetic song of the Lord (Lk. 1:39-56).

The prophetess Anna was the first person to publicly preach Christ after His birth (Lk. 2:36-38).

Joanna and Susanna "ministered" to Jesus from their possessions (Lk. 8:1-3; 23:55; 24:10). This is the Greek word from which we get the English word "deacon."

Mary and Martha, sisters to Lazarus, opened their home and their hearts to the Lord (Lk. 10:38-42).

Mary Magdalene (there is no proof she was a prostitute), the first witness of His resurrection, was the woman who fell in love with Jesus (see Mt. 27:56,61; 28:1; Mk. 16:1,9; Jn. 20:18). Some Church fathers called her the apostle to the apostles!

The Great Commission promises that supernatural signs and wonders would follow "them" (men and women) who believe (Mk. 16:15-20). Moreover, the Book of Acts abounds with the ministry of women.

There were women, along with Mary the mother of Jesus, who were boldly praying alongside the men in the upper room. These daughters and handmaids were subsequently filled with the Holy Ghost and publicly declared the wonderful works of God (Acts 1:13-15; 2:1-11).

The apostle Peter announced that New Testament women would prophesy, fulfilling Joel's prediction (Joel 2:28-32, with Acts 2:17-18). Despite persecution, women received mighty infillings of the Holy Spirit and spoke the Word of God with boldness (Acts 4:23-31).

Christian women were unmercifully dragged from their homes and imprisoned for the sake of their gospel witness (Acts 8:3).

The disciple Dorcas, the noted servant and famous dressmaker from Joppa, was raised from the dead by the apostle Peter (Acts 9:36-43).

When Peter was delivered from prison, he went straight to the house church of Mary. It was there that the damsel Rhoda believed when all the men had no faith (Acts 12:12-17).

Lydia, Paul's first Philippian convert, was the famous businesswoman who assisted the apostle in his ministry (Acts 16:12-15,40; Phil. 1:1-10).

The women of Berea were ardent students of the Scriptures (Acts 17:10-12).

Priscilla (sometimes mentioned first because of her prominence) worked with her husband Aquila to "expound" the way of God more accurately to the great teacher Apollos. This same word is used to describe the public ministries of the two central figures of the Book of Acts, Peter and Paul (Acts 18:2,18,24-26; see also Acts 11:4; 28:23). Aquila and Priscilla co-pastored a church in their house, and she is also called Paul's "helper" or "colaborer" (Rom. 16:3; 1 Cor. 16:19; compare 2 Cor. 8:23; Phil. 2:25).

The evangelist Philip had four daughters who prophesied (Acts 21:9). It is possible that these prophetic women traveled and evangelized as a family team.

We have noted examples from the four Gospels and the Book of Acts. What do the Pauline and general Epistles say about women's ministry?

At no place in Paul's writings does the apostle prohibit the sisters from ministering to men and women in the local church under proper covering or from proclaiming the gospel to men and women outside the Church with proper attitudes of submission.

Phebe was a "servant" or "deaconess" at Cenchrea (Rom. 16:1-2). This dignified, wealthy woman of rank stood before many and served. She is called a "succourer"; this Greek word is *prostatis*, which means "to stand before (in rank), to preside"—a presiding officer or elder. The fame of Phebe was spread abroad as she traveled and ministered. As previously noted, she carried Paul's Epistle to the Roman church.

Can a husband and wife constitute an apostolic team? Many believe that Junia was a woman (and the wife of Andronicus), not a man, and therefore a notable apostle (Rom. 16:7). Whether the gender of the original is masculine (*Junias*) or feminine (*Junia*) is not certain. The word "kinsmen" of this passage is *suggenes* and means "a relative by blood." It is a compound of *sun* ("with") and *genos* ("kin"). John Chrysostom (337-407), bishop of Constantinople, said of Junia, "Oh, how great is the devotion of this woman that she should be counted worthy of the appellation of apostle."[1] Origen of Alexandria said that the name was a variant of Julia, mentioned in Romans 16:15, as does Thayer's Lexicon.[2]

The identity of Junia as a female apostle was not questioned until the Middle Ages. Translators tried to change the gender of the name to the masculine form, *Junias*. Leonard Swidler cited Jerome and Peter Abelard as believing Junia to be a woman; he stated, "To the best of my knowledge, no commentator on the text until Aegius of Rome (1245-1316) took the name to be masculine."[3]

Mary, along with Tryphena and Tyrphosa, labored with Paul in the Lord (Rom. 16:6,12).

Pastor Chloe's people reported to Paul (1 Cor. 1:11).

Paul said that women could pray or prophesy publicly (1 Cor. 11:5,13). However the words are interpreted "praying and prophesying" in respect to the man, they have precisely the same meaning in respect to the woman.

"To one" and to "another" (not just to a man) are bestowed the supernatural manifestations of the Spirit; they are given to "all" (1 Cor. 12:4-10).

By comparing Paul's writings, we could say that by one Spirit have we all been baptized into one Body, whether male or female (1 Cor. 12:13 with Gal. 3:28).

Euodias and Synteche labored with Paul in the "gospel," or the *evangel* (Phil. 4:1-3).

Some translations render "Nymphas" as "Nympha," in reference to the person who had a church in his/her house (Col. 4:15). It is not certain Paul was writing in regard to a man or a woman.

Paul used the feminine form of *presbuteros*, the Greek word for "elder," in describing the "elder women" and the "aged women" (1 Tim. 5:2; Tit. 2:3-5).

When Paul gave the qualifications for the office of the "bishop" (overseer or elder), his introductory statement leaves this office wide open to both sexes! He wrote in First Timothy 3:1, "If a man [*tis*] desire the office of a bishop...."

Tis is an indefinite pronoun, which means "anyone," male or female, someone or certain one, usually meaning both sexes. If the Lord wanted only males for this office, Paul would have used *aner*, the unmistakable word for "man." *Tis* is used generically throughout the New Testament (as in Mt. 11:27; Lk. 9:23; Jn. 6:51; 7:17,37; 8:52;

12:26; 14:23; 15:13; Acts 4:34; 9:2; 2 Tim. 2:5,21; Heb. 4:1; Jas. 1:5; 1 Jn. 2:1,15,27). It was specifically used by Jesus to designate those who are born of water and the Spirit, of whom He later said, "He that receiveth *whomsoever* [*tis*] I send receiveth Me…" (Jn. 3:3,5; 13:20a).

Paul gave qualifications for deaconesses; "even so" (1 Tim. 3:11a) is the Greek word *hosautos*. It means "in the same way or manner, likewise."

Eunice and Lois, Timothy's source of unfeigned faith, were his mother and grandmother (Acts 16:1-3; 2 Tim. 1:5; 3:14-15).

Apphia was a close friend of Paul and Timothy (Philem. 2).

The "elect lady" and the "elect sister" were terms that may have been addressed to a female overseer or church officer (2 Jn. 1,13). "Lady" is from the Greek word *kuria*, the feminine form of "lord, master." It might also be "Cyria" (her name), transliterated from the original language.

Jezebel was a false prophetess and teacher in the Church at Thyratira who was given space to repent of her fornication, not her teaching ministry (Rev. 2:20-21).

The Unsung Heroines

Besides the many famous women mentioned by name throughout the Old and New Testaments, there are many more who are unnamed.

Noah's wife and his sons' wives stepped out of the ark to rule the earth with their husbands (Gen. 6–8).

The Hebrew midwives fearlessly brought forth a mighty nation in spite of the Pharaoh who knew not Joseph (Ex. 1:15-21).

Pharaoh's daughter providentially adopted the baby Moses (Ex. 2:5-10; Acts 7:21; Heb. 11:24).

Wisehearted women helped to fashion the Mosaic Tabernacle (Ex. 35:22-29; 36:1-3).

A company of women assembled by troops at the door of the Tabernacle to minister unto the Lord (Ex. 38:8).

There were many priestly daughters (Lev. 21:9).

Women could take the Nazirite vow of separation (Num. 6:2).

The heroine of Thebez slew the wicked judge Abimelech (Judg. 9:50-57; 2 Sam. 11:21).

Manoah's wife was the mother of Samson (Judg. 13:1–14:5; Heb. 11:32).

The wise woman of Tekoah was renowned (2 Sam. 14:1-20).

The wise woman of Abel was equally famous (2 Sam. 20:16-22).

The mother of Hiram, the man who helped David build Solomon's Temple, was probably a notable businesswoman (2 Chron. 2:13-14).

The wealthy Queen of Sheba sought after wisdom (1 Kings 10).

The widow of Zarephath sustained the great prophet Elijah (1 Kings 17:8-24; Lk. 4:25-26).

The mother of the prophet Elisha birthed and nurtured God's man of restoration (1 Kings 19:20).

The woman of Shunem was great (2 Kings 4:8-37; 8:1-6).

The three daughters of Heman publicly sang in the house of the Lord (1 Chron. 25:5-6).

Singing women ministered with the Levites (2 Chron. 35:25). Psalms 8 and 45 may have been originally intended for women's voices alone.

Female construction workers helped their father Shallum repair Jerusalem's city walls (Neh. 3:12).

The three daughters of the early patriarch Job— Jemima, Kezia, and Keren-Happuch— all received an inheritance among their brothers (Job 42:13-15).

Isaiah's wife was a prophetess (Is. 8:1-4).

Jeremiah's mother brought forth an international weeping prophet (Jer. 15:20).

Ezekiel's wife was a most unique and patient woman, giving the ultimate sacrifice (Ezek. 24:15-27).

In the New Testament, Peter's wife and mother-in-law are both mentioned but not named (Mt. 8:14-18; Mk. 1:29-34; Lk. 4:38-41).

The woman with the issue of blood was healed by Jesus after she pressed through a crowd of men (Mt. 9:20-22; Mk. 5:25-34; Lk. 8:43-48).

Jairus' daughter was raised from the dead (Mt. 9:18-25; Mk. 5:21-43; Lk. 8:41-56).

Jesus had natural sisters born to Joseph and Mary (Mt. 13:55-56; Mk. 6:3).

The Syrophoenican woman believed Jesus to heal her daughter (Mt. 15:21-28; Mk. 7:24-30).

The women at Calvary were faithful when the apostles fled (Mt. 27:55).

The widow with two mites gave all (Mk. 12:41-44; Lk. 21:1-4).

The widow of Nain's son was raised from the dead (Lk. 7:11-18).

The woman of Samaria became the first female evangelist in the New Testament; her ministry laid the foundation for Philip's citywide revival in Samaria (Jn. 4; Acts 8).

The woman taken in adultery was forgiven (Jn. 8:1-11).

Women met with Paul down by the river side (Acts 16:13).

Paul had a natural sister (Acts 23:16-22).

The mother of Rufus (the son of Simon of Cyrene, who carried Jesus' cross) was like a mother to Paul (Rom. 16:13; see also Mk. 15:21).

Such is the vast scope of women's ministry throughout the Scriptures as revealed in the law, the Psalms, and the prophets of the Old Testament; the Gospels, the Book of Acts, and the Epistles of the New Testament. Let God's Word be true!

But what can be said about women in the record of Church history?

Chapter Five

The Public Ministry
of Women Throughout
Church History

"And I will restore to you the years...."

Joel 2:25

God has given us history for our minds and the Scriptures for our hearts, or spirits. These corroborating witnesses form the cement of an unshakeable foundation. Chapter Four of this work examined the biblical record. But what does Church history say about the public ministry of women?

The period between A.D. 100 and 1000 is known as the Patristic period. These "fathers," along with the rulings of the first Church councils, did for Christianity what rabbinicism did for Judaism. Many of these persons were outspokenly negative toward women and worked to exclude them from all church service. It's unfortunate that many contemporary leaders quote some of these fathers as their source and authority for silencing women in the Church.

The Fathers are divided into two groups of men, the Latin Fathers and the Greek Fathers. The Latin Fathers include Tertullian, Ambrose, Jerome, Augustine, and Gregory the Great. The Greek Fathers include Clement of Alexandria, Origen, Dionysius the Great, John Chrysostom, Epiphanium, and Cyril of Alexandria. There were many others, but the men noted above were the most prolific writers of these groups. A brief look at some of their works will reveal a gradual shift away from biblical truth into religious confusion and tradition.

Clement (150–215) headed the Catechetical School of Alexandria. He is often associated with the Gnostics, who distrusted the physical body. His writings reveal a magnificent intelligence and reasoning ability, but he apparently was insecure about his own masculinity. He wrote, "Man is stronger and purer since he is uncastrated and has a beard. Women are weak, passive, castrated, and immature...."[1]

Origen (185–254), one of Clement's students, succeeded him as the head of the school at Alexandria. He also was influenced by Gnosticism, the philosophical dualism which taught that the spirit was pure while the flesh was evil and earthly. To Origen, women were the opposite of spirit. Some of his writings were bent toward the philosophies of the ancient rabbis, "It is not proper for a woman to speak in church, however admirable or holy what she says may be, merely because it comes from female lips."[2]

Tertullian (160–225) was the first Latin father. He was a prolific, polemical writer whose works are second only to those of Augustine. According to Jerome, Tertullian left the priesthood and joined the Montanists, who discouraged marriage. This continued to influence his thinking. Many of his lectures were anti-woman, and, like the rabbis, he blamed Eve for bringing sin and death into the world: "You are the devil's gateway, you are the unsealer of that [forbidden] tree; you are the first deserter of the divine law; you are she who persuaded him whom the devil was not valiant enough to attack. You destroyed so easily God's image, man."[3]

Ambrose (340–397), bishop of Milan, was instrumental in the conversion of Augustine. Like the Judaizers, Ambrose believed women to be inferior to men and, influenced by Gnosticism, related them to the flesh. Like the Greek Church Fathers, he considered women equal to men after conversion. He said, "Thus woman is inferior to man, she is part of him, she is under his command. Sin began with her, she must wear the sign, the veil."[4]

Augustine (354–430) was a clever, clear thinker who has been credited with laying the groundwork for a Roman Catholic theology that lasted for a millennium. His *City of God* is still considered a classic. After his conversion, the Gnostic idea of dualism surfaced, which labeled man the superior spirit while woman was again likened to inferior flesh. He taught that flesh stands for the woman and the spirit for the husband; the latter rules and the former is ruled. He proclaimed that woman stands under the lordship of man and possesses no authority to teach or be a witness. His only proof was the oral law of the Jews.

These famous patricians were products of the thinking of the age in which they lived and studied. As a result there was a progressive decline of women's rank and acceptance in the Church after the middle of the second century. The influence of Judaism is discernable in many areas of this tradition, especially in regard to the hierarchical structure of the Church. The Fathers adapted the Jewish male-superior attitude, following the same faulty reasoning based on untruths, superstitions, and other prejudices. Most were celibates with a distaste for marriage. By the fifth century, the Church's mistrust and misunderstanding of women was complete—women were back in bondage again.

The concept that every believer is a priest or minister was exchanged for a professional priesthood. The Holy Spirit was systematically shut out of the public services, and His people were excluded from all ministry. By the time of Augustine, the ordination of priests had become a sacrament, and the ministry was the exclusive right of the sacerdotal priesthood. The ministries of both lay men and women disappeared. Because there was no provision for women priests in ancient Israel, it seemed natural to exclude them from New Testament ministry. As noted, the Church Fathers assumed that God was male and bearded. Therefore they felt that all His representatives should be male.

Records reveal that the Western Church continued to ordain women deacons well into the second century, while the Eastern Church continued the practice into the fourth century. At first there were apostolic constitutions in which bishops were charged to ordain women deacons, "Ordain also a women deacon who is faithful and holy."[5] During the second century, apostles passed from the historical stage and apostasy set in. Women's ministries began to change, especially with the rise of Romism in the Western Church.

The Council of Orange convened in A.D. 441 and directed, "Let no one proceed to the ordination of deaconesses anymore."[6] Seventy-five years later, the Council of Opaon decreed in Canon 21, "We abrogate completely in the entire kingdom the consecration of widows who are named deaconesses." Sixteen years later, the Council of Orleans took the Church all the way back to the traditions of the Jewish elders: "No longer shall the blessing of women deaconesses be given, because of the weakness of the sex."[7] Rabbinical traditions and human assumptions were not only accepted by the Church leaders; they were being taught as truth.

We can but briefly comment on the outstanding women of Church history between A.D. 500–1400. Such a list would include the following examples:[8]

Early catacomb paintings have been found showing women in the authoritative stance of a bishop, conferring blessings upon Christians of both sexes. Frescoes in the Cappella Greca of the catacomb of Priscilla show seven women serving communion. A similar fresco from the same catacomb shows women with hands upraised leading prayer in group services. Another fresco from third century Rome shows what may be a woman in the role of a bishop, blessing pastors in her charge.

Many historians allude to Thecla, an apostle and associate of Paul, whose ministry became noted in Asia Minor. Their story is recorded in the second century manuscript, "The Acts of Paul and Thecla." She founded a teaching center and hospital near Seleucia (the port of Syrian Antioch from which Paul embarked on his first missionary journey), which remained in active use for 1,000 years.

Catherine of Alexandria, the patron saint of scholars and philosophers, lived in the second century. She allegedly debated 50 philosophers and won them all to Christ, for which she was martyred on the wheel.

Marcella (325–410) established the first convent for women in the Western Church. Jerome taught the Bible to the women of Rome in her oratory. When the Goths sacked Rome, they beat her, attempting to make her reveal the hiding place of her fortune, but she had already given it to the poor.

Anthusa of Antioch in Syria (347–407) was the devout mother and tutor of John Chrysostom, one of the greatest leaders and preachers of the fourth-century Church.

Candace, Queen of Ethiopia, converted by the eunuch (Acts 8:27), used her influence to promote Christianity in her nation and the surrounding countries.

Paula (347–404) was a close friend, inspirer, and supporter of the scholar Jerome, who translated the Old Testament from Greek to Latin (the Vulgate). She helped with the work of translation and later, with her converts, copied the manuscripts.

Brigid of Ireland (450–523), said to have been consecrated as a bishop, founded Ireland's first nunnery and spread Christianity there.

Hilda, the Anglo-Saxon abbess of Whitby (614–680), founded an English monastery that trained five bishops and hosted the Synod of Whitby. Kings and rulers sought her advice.

Lioba (700–780) helped her cousin Boniface, the apostle to the Germans, to convert the Saxons. She was a ruler, teacher, and expositor.

Hrotsvit (932–1002), a German Christian woman, wrote verse, history, and composed the first known dramas in Church history.

Queen Margaret of Scotland (1046–1093) vigorously reformed the church.

The Waldensians, a group beginning in the twelfth century who have been described as "Protestants before the Reformation," were charged with allowing women to preach.

Anna Comnena (1083–1150), daughter of Byzantine Emperor Alexius I, wrote the most detailed history of the Church of her time.

Clare (1194–1253), a co-worker with Francis of Assisi, took the vow of poverty and organized the Franciscan Order of Poor Clares, a religious order for women that spread throughout the world.

Elizabeth of Hungary (1207–1231), daughter of a king, wife and mother of princes, used her royal revenue to aid the distressed. During a famine she fed 900 at her palace gate. She built a hospital and cared for the sick.

Teenage Joan of Arc (1412–1431), called the Deborah of France, declared she had heard from God that she was to lead the besieged French forces to victory against England during the latter part of the Hundred

Years War. She was later burned at the stake on charges of heresy.

There were many more famous women who lived just prior to and during the Protestant Reformation and its consequent missionary endeavors.[9] Queen Isabella of Spain (1451–1504) financed Columbus' first voyage to America for religious reasons. On his second voyage she sent clergy and equipment for the first church in the new world. Her ten-year crusade against Moslem Moors had a Christian objective.

Vittoria Colonna (1490–1547), one of the greatest spirits of the Italian Renaissance, increased Michelangelo's faith and inspired the great artist with an ideal of womanhood. Together, they worked for reform within the Church, she with her pen and he with his chisel. She is the first woman in history to use her talents to write religious verse.

Margaret, Queen of Navarre (1492–1549), sister of King Francis I of France, gave refuge to French Reformers in her palace, becoming a godmother of the Reformation.

Katherine Von Bora (1499–1552) became the wife of Martin Luther. The Proverbs ideal of a wife and mother, she was the matriarch of the Protestant parsonage.

Anne Hutchinson (1591–1643) arrived in the Massachusetts Bay Colony in 1634. Mother to 16 children, she also became the first woman preacher in New England. The spirit of this fearless defender of religious freedom survived her persecution and death.

Pocahontas (1595–1617), wife of John Rolfe, was the first Indian woman to become a Christian at the English settlement of Jamestown.

Margaret Fell Fox (1614–1702) was the wife of George Fox, founder of the Quaker movement. Her home, Swarthmoor Hall, served as a focal point for the early work of the Quakers, whom she guided, befriended, and inspired during the first half-century of their history.

Madame Guyon of France (1648–1717) influenced Catholics and Protestants throughout Europe during her eight-year apostolic pilgrimage through France and Switzerland. Imprisoned in the Bastille for her beliefs, she wrote 40 books, including a 20-volume commentary on the Bible.

Susanna Wesley (1669–1742) was the mother of 19 children. Her fifteenth child was John, the founder of Methodism; her eighteenth was Charles, the great hymn writer.

Selina (1707–1791), Countess of Huntingdon and a revivalist, founded the evangelical branch known as Lady Huntingdon's Connexion, and inspired early Methodist leaders John and Charles Wesley and George Whitefield. She sponsored about 60 chapels in the British Isles, financed a seminary for ministers, and aided in the establishment of missions in Georgia.

"Mother Ann" Lee (1736–1784) joined the Shaking Quakers in England in 1758 and established the first Shaker colony in the United States of America.

Ann Judson (1789–1826), wife of Adoniram Judson, was the first American woman missionary to the Far East. She assisted him in translating the Bible into Burmese and wrote a history of the Burma Mission.

Narcissa Whitman (1808–1847), missionary to the Indians, established the first mission home in the Pacific

Northwest. She taught and mothered homeless frontier children.

Dorothea Lynde Dix (1802–1887), a saint known for work in medicine and philanthropy, was cited for her work as superintendent of nurses in the Union Army during the Civil War.

Florence Nightingale (1820–1910), the heroine of modern nursing, was the ministering angel of the Crimean War.

Harriet Tubman (1820–1913), called the "Moses" of her people, escaped slavery and then began working to eventually free some 300 slaves. She claimed to be led and guided by God through visions and dreams.

Elizabeth Blackwell (1821–1910), the first woman doctor in America, later opened a school for her female colleagues.

Quaker Sarah Grimke entered the movement for women's rights and abolition of slavery. She encouraged women to exercise leadership and become visible on relevant issues.

Catherine Booth (1829–1890), wife of William Booth and mother of eight children, helped establish the Christian Mission and the Salvation Army (1861). She was considered the most popular preacher of her time.

Antoinette L. Brown (1825–1921), a convert of Charles Finney (who encouraged women to speak in mixed assemblies), was the first American woman to be ordained a minister. This took place at the Congregational Church of South Butler, New York, on September 15, 1853. At the time of her death, 68 years after her ordination, there were more than 3,000 women ministers in the United States.

Phoebe Palmer, an associate evangelist with D.L. Moody, was credited with the conversion of 25,000 souls.

Katherine Bushnell (1856–1946) was a medical doctor and a learned scholar in Hebrew and Greek. She pioneered the Anchorage Mission in Chicago, housing up to 5,000 women per year. She ministered extensively in India and continued her research in England. Upon her return to the United States, this powerful teacher wrote her classic, *God's Word to Women*, published in 1923.

Maria Woodworth-Etter was a great Pentecostal forerunner. Born in 1844, she began to minister the gospel in her mid-twenties. By the 1880s (and before her personal Pentecostal experience), she was preaching to tent crowds of 20,000 or more. She pioneered dozens of churches and licensed other preachers, pastoring in Indianapolis from 1918 until her death in 1924. Her life and ministry is documented in her book, *A Diary of Signs and Wonders*.[10]

Hannah Whitall Smith (1832–1911), author of *The Christian's Secret of a Happy Life* (1875), catalyzed the development of the holiness movement in Britain and throughout Europe. Her activities in England led to the founding of the Keswick Convention in 1874. Later, the great Christian author Jessie Penn-Lewis also became an important Keswick leader.

The year 1901 was a landmark. The restoration of the reality of the Pentecostal experience at the turn of this century, more than any other event, liberated women and restored them to their God-ordained New Testament ministry in the Body of Christ. Once the power of the Holy Ghost took precedent over the reasoning of men, the One who wrote the Bible began to explain it.

During this awakening, the determined basis for authority to preach began to rest upon the individual's anointing from the Spirit, and great emphasis was placed upon the call of God. Out of the Holiness movement, which ordained women pastors, came many social reforms, especially the idea of correspondent rights for all. There were many notable female Pentecostal pioneers.[11]

At the turn of this century, under the direction of Charles F. Parham, founder of Bethel Bible School in Topeka, Kansas, students studied the Scriptures concerning the evidence of the baptism of the Holy Spirit. Soon they discovered the biblical record of other "tongues" (Acts 2:4; 10:46; 19:6). On New Year's Day, 1901, Agnes N. Ozman asked Brother Parham first to lay hands on her so that she would be filled with the Holy Spirit. This young pioneer began speaking in the Chinese language and was unable to speak in English for three days. She later answered the call of God to become an evangelist.

Charles Parham and William Seymour were associated with many women of great anointing and leadership, among whom were Mary Arthur, Lucy Farrow, Anna Hall, and Florence Crawford. Parham's daughter-in-law, Pauline Parham, was one of the first Spirit-filled women ministers. She preached and pastored four independent Pentecostal churches and started three Bible schools.

Amanda Smith (1839–1915), born a slave, became one of the most influential, widely traveled, and respected black holiness evangelists of the nineteenth century, preaching in England, Scotland, India, Africa, and other parts of the world. Her autobiography deeply impacted Charles H. Mason, who served under William Seymour at the Azusa Street revival, and who later founded the Church of God in Christ (1907), the oldest Pentecostal denomination on record. Some said of Amanda Smith that she was "God's image carved in ebony."

Lizzie Roberson (1860–1945), a brilliant organizer, was the first national supervisor of women in the Church of God in Christ.

In the same era, Helen Barrett Montgomery (1861–1934), was the only woman to translate the Greek New Testament into English. A licensed minister, she was the first woman to serve as the president of the Northern Baptist Convention.

Alice Belle Garrigus (1858–1949) was the founding mother of the Pentecostal Assemblies of Newfoundland.

Alice Reynolds Flower (born in 1890), was a pioneer leader in the Assemblies of God along with her husband J. Roswell Flower. They founded the *Pentecostal Evangel* (then *Christian Evangel*) in 1913. A mother of six children, five of whom became ordained ministers, her devotional writings have made a major contribution to the literature of Pentecostal spirituality.

Zelma Argue (1900–1980) was a well-known Pentecostal evangelist and teacher, the eldest daughter of A.H. Argue, with whom she travelled extensively during the 1920s and 1930s. She was ordained by the Assemblies of God in 1920; and, being a prolific writer, she contributed more than 200 articles to *The Pentecostal Evangel*, their national publication.

Marie Brown (1880–1971) pastored Glad Tidings Tabernacle in New York with her husband George. She had been sent there earlier as an evangelist by Charles Parham. This church led the Assemblies of God in missionary giving in the 1920s through the 1940s. After her husband's death in 1948, Marie pastored the church until her death in 1971.

Carrie Judd Montgomery (1858–1946) was a minister, teacher, writer, editor, director of faith homes, and social worker whose ministry spanned more than 65 years. She was known worldwide for her magazine, *Triumphs of Faith*.

Aimee Semple McPherson (1890–1944), founder of the Church of the Foursquare Gospel and the Lighthouse for International Foursquare Evangelism (L.I.F.E.) Bible College (1923), preached evangelistic messages across the country while serving as the senior pastor of Angeles Temple. She preached up to 21 times a week, wrote 180 songs, 13 dramas, and 7 full-length sacred operas. Thousands were drawn to her healing ministry. She was the first woman to receive an FCC license to operate a radio station, KFSG (1924).

Kathryn Kuhlman (1907–1976) began preaching in the 1920s and continued her charismatic ministry for more than 50 years. In 1972 she received the first honorary doctorate awarded by Oral Roberts University. Her miracle ministry is discussed in her book, *I Believe in Miracles.*[12]

Christine Gibson (1879–1955), educator, pastor, and champion of the faith principle, headed the Zion Bible

Institute, East Providence, Rhode Island, during the first 31 years of its existence.

Myrtle Beall (1896–1979) founded and pastored Bethesda Missionary Temple in Detroit, Michigan. Her church became a center, a spiritual armory, for the 1948 Latter Rain movement, attracting thousands of visitors. Her daughter, Patricia Beall Gruitts, wrote the classic catechism *Understanding God* (1962).

Daisy Osborn, along with her husband, T.L. Osborn, began their internationally known overseas ministry in 1948. By 1964 they had ministered in over 40 countries. Her many responsibilities included being international editor of *Faith Digest* magazine.

Singer Maude Aimee Humbard, along with her preacher husband Pastor Rex Humbard of the Cathedral of Tomorrow, Akron, Ohio, helped to pioneer the ministry of Christian television.

Freda Lindsay and her husband Gordan Lindsay were leaders of the healing movement, editors, publishers (the first issue of *The Voice of Healing* was published in 1948), founders and directors of Christ for the Nations Institute. Following her husband's death in 1973, Freda took over the leadership of the school and its enterprises.

The Charismatic renewal of the 1960s and 1970s produced many outstanding women teachers, such as Gloria Copeland, Marilyn Hickey, and Joyce Myers.

Rita Francis, better known as Mother Angelica, experienced a spiritual renewal in the early 1970s, and later (1981) boldly launched the Eternal Word Television Network (EWTN), the first Catholic satellite cable network.

"Mother" Eleanor Workman, veteran missionary to the island of Haiti, answered the call of God in 1970 at the age of 51. Through faith and prayer alone, she has raised up a ministry that feeds and educates more than 500 children each day.

Nobel Prize winner Mother Teresa has done incredible work in the name of Jesus to unite people of all denominations and beliefs to work on behalf of the poor, the sick, and the underprivileged.

From the 1950s until the present, God has accelerated His purposes in restoration. As God is re-establishing the fivefold ministry, some have observed certain emphases within these time frames:

1. The 1950s— the restoration of the evangelists.

2. The 1960s— the restoration of the pastors/ shepherds.

3. The 1970s— the restoration of the teachers.

4. The 1980s— the restoration of the prophets.

5. The 1990s— the restoration of the apostles.

My *personal* life and ministry have been blessed and impacted by ongoing relationships with outstanding, contemporary women ministers and notable prophetesses, among whom the following can be listed:

Lora Allison, Lorraine Alston, Barbara Amos, Sue Baird, Charlotte Baker, Mary Ann Brown, Joanne Bunce, Sandra Clements, Lynn Daniel, Clarice Fluitt, Betty Forbes, Anne Gimenez, the late Ione Glaeser, Jane Hamon, Vivian Hibbert, Violet

Kitely, Patricia Morgan, Fucshia Pickett, Janet Shell, Kluane Spake, and Iverna Thompkins.

When asked to succinctly summarize the truth about the issue of contemporary women's ministry in the Body of Christ, some of these women said:

"God is going to deal with all prejudice—if a man or woman is truly called of God, that gift will make room for him/her."

"I don't believe in women preachers. I don't believe in men preachers. I believe in Holy Ghost-anointed preachers."

"Women are still being told that they must suffer for the sin of Eve. It is amazing that the Church seems to believe that the blood of Jesus cannot eradicate that curse!"

"When faith comes, prejudice leaves."

"Men are not sexist enemies of women. The culprit is the enmity of satan."

"The issue is, 'What did God say?' not what man says that God says."

"God does not require that we be accepted by others, only that we be stewards who are faithful."

"Any identity apart from the quickened life of our Lord Jesus Christ is but chaff."

"There is no prejudice in the realm of spirit— the love of God has swallowed it up."

"We must refuse to know anyone, male or female, except through the cross."

"This worldwide discrimination based on sex must be challenged."

"The body is nothing but an exterior garment. The spirit, the essence on the inside, is made in the image of God and is neither male or female."

"When it came to serving mankind, Jesus brought redemption to all. Where women are concerned, Jesus raised their standard of respect by His demonstration."

"Jesus was the original 'women's Liberator'! His attitude toward women was positive and endorsing. He defended women against the false rabbinical interpretation, social traditions, and prejudices of His day. He accepted women as qualified equals to men in all things. He fulfilled the Old Covenant and gave us a New Covenant where there is neither Jew nor Greek, male nor female, bond nor free—in Christ. Nowhere in the Bible does the Lord forbid women from serving God in whatever capacity He ordains them to fulfill. My prayer is for the Church to embrace this same attitude."

Prejudice against gender is a religious spirit based upon the wrong understanding and application of the Scriptures. Despite the many powerful biblical and historical examples already examined, two primary New Testament Pauline passages have been wrongly used to keep women in a legalistic straitjacket for 2,000 years. It is now time to fearlessly re-examine them.

Chapter Six

The Pauline Passages

"...Thy word is truth."

John 17:17

We have sampled the biblical and historical record with regard to the public ministry of women. In light of the truth that Jesus came to liberate women into life, liberty, and ministry, along with all the New Testament evidence of public women's ministry, did Paul intentionally contradict all this with two sentences? The apostle has gotten a bad rap on this issue.

Was Paul a bitter old bachelor who disliked women and felt threatened by them? Did two brief verses from Paul's Epistles sew up the veil that Jesus rent and bind women again to the law of sin and death?

There are only two biblical limitations to the vast ministry of women (note: men give more restrictions than does the Head of the Church)! First, in learning the Word, the woman is to be quiet; in receiving, she is to be silent. Second, in ministering the Word, the woman is to be covered; in giving, she is to be submissive, under authority to her husband and the local church eldership. That's it! So why is sexual prejudice still so prevalent in the Body of Christ? Let's take another look at what Paul really said in the two passages referred to above. The first passage is found in Paul's letter to the church at Corinth:

1 Cor. 14:34-35, KJV

Let your women keep silence in the churches: for it is not permitted unto them to speak; but they are commanded to be under obedience, as also saith the law.

And if they will learn any thing, let them ask their husbands at home: for it is a shame for women to speak in the church.

Isolated, these verses could be interpreted to mean that no woman can play an instrument, make a prayer request, give an announcement, preach, greet a visitor, calm a baby, or even cough in the house of the Lord! But the apostle had just said in First Corinthians 14:31 that all (male and female) could and should prophesy.

Chapters 11 through 14 of First Corinthians provide instructions for the meeting together of believers in the public assembly: Chapter 11 emphasizes the foundation of Jesus Christ, which is to be remembered in the breaking of bread; chapter 12 describes the flow of spiritual gifts and the unity of the Body of Christ; chapter 13 reveals the love of God, the fellowship and motivation of public gatherings; and chapter 14 highlights the function of the Holy Spirit in the operation of spiritual gifts for the edification of all.

God is not the author of confusion or disorder. Bitterness, envy, and carnal wisdom that comes from prejudiced brethren have fostered much frustration and strife in the Body. We need the wisdom that comes from above and is without partiality.

When Paul said, "Let your women keep silence in the churches...," to whom was he speaking? This Greek word for "women" is *gune*, found 221 times in the New Testament. It means "a woman, married or unmarried," and it is translated in the King James Version as "wife, wives, woman." The immediate context of this first key passage indicates that the "women" Paul is referring to were married; they were women who had husbands. The parallel text in First Timothy 2:11-12, the second passage under examination in this chapter, likewise refers to "women" with husbands.

These married women were not to keep completely silent in the Church, for Paul had already encouraged them to pray and prophesy. Furthermore, the plural Greek word *adelphoi* translated as "brethren" in First Corinthians 14:26 refers to a community based on identity of origin or life— a group of brothers *and* sisters. In other words, men *and* women could bring a song, a word of instruction, a revelation, a tongue and interpretation.

Wives are to keep silence, or hold their peace, only while receiving or learning. That is the sole dimension in which they are not permitted or allowed to speak. That is the only context in which they are to be under obedience or subordinate in the local assembly. While receiving instruction the married woman is to rank herself under her husband and the local elders. The parallel cross-reference in First Timothy 2:11 declares that the married woman is to learn in silence with all subjection.

In one respect alone (in receiving) is the woman to keep quiet in the Church. She is not to keep silence all the time. Get the principle, not the letter. Her speaking out in this context would reflect upon her husband and show a lack of confidence in his priesthood in the home. The woman needs to defer to her husband in public. Some women have shattered their husbands' confidence by appealing to more spiritual men. Don't become a legalist with these truths. Paul was after an attitude, a spirit that was in certain married women who did not want to submit to their husbands or the local church leadership. Preachers who do not understand the context of these Scriptures demand that women keep quiet in the public assembly—period. Such self-righteousness needs an adjusted vision.

Jesus has redeemed women from the curse, but there is still a divine order. When learning, wives (and husbands, too) need to maintain the attitudes and actions of a meek and quiet spirit. When men and women will not submit to one another in the fear of the Lord, there will be confusion and every evil work.

Moreover, the Pauline phrase "as also saith the law" in First Corinthians 14:34 is most interesting. In that day, Judaizers were bringing circumcision and other Jewish traditions into the Church. Their oral traditions (the *Mishna*) eventually evolved into an interpretive collection of books and commentaries compiled by Jewish rabbis from A.D. 250-500: the Talmud (which means "study" or "learning").

The Talmud declared, "It is a shame for a woman to let her voice be heard among men; women are but made to bear children." These Jewish writings further stated that the testimony of 100 women is not equal to that of one man! But what about the testimony of one woman in the fourth chapter of John? Another example from the Talmud is the "wisdom" of Rabbi Eleazer: "Let the words of the law be burned than rather they should be delivered to a woman." But we have already noted that the apostle Paul entrusted his great Epistle of Romans to a woman deaconness, Phebe; and Jesus entrusted a woman to be the first messenger of His resurrection—Mary Magdalene.

Moreover, there is not one verse of Scripture in the entire Old Testament that says, "For it is not permitted unto them to speak...." Where did the law say that in the Old Testament? There is not one trace of those words from Genesis to Malachi!

The fifth through fourteenth chapters of First Corinthians were answers given by the apostle in reply to the Corinthian inquiry. Many maintain (including this author) that Paul was referencing the traditions of the Judaizers (the oral law) here in First Corinthians 14:34-35, which prohibited women from speaking. The phrase, "it is not permitted" therefore points to Jewish tradition ("it," the oral law) that forbade women to speak. The apostle was quoting the Judaizers at Corinth. Paul stated elsewhere that New Testament believers are delivered from the law and that we should serve God in the newness of the Spirit, not the oldness of the letter.

So wives are to keep silence while receiving. Paul adds that if they wish, or desire, to "learn" something, they should ask or question their own husbands in the home. This word means to learn as a disciple, to learn by inquiry and observation. Otherwise, it is a shame or a disgraceful thing to speak out those questions in the public assembly. Paul used the same word to describe a woman who is not covered, thus dishonoring her head or husband (1 Cor. 11:3-6; see also Eph. 5:12).

Married women are to ask their own "husbands" at home. This is *aner*, the Greek word for "husband." It is translated as "man" in First Timothy 2:12.

Paul went on to say in First Corinthians 14:37-38 that we should "acknowledge" these principles as the Word of the Lord. This word means "to know fully, accurately, thoroughly." We are to fully perceive and discern these matters. The commandment of the Lord is contrasted with the traditions of men. But if men (Judaizers, then and now) still disagree with truth, the apostle said to leave them in their ignorance. According to First Corinthians 14:39, no one is to forbid by their words and actions any woman to speak with tongues, or to speak at all.

Other considerations can be made with regard to the Corinthian passage. Some simply treat this passage as an apostolic injunction against women chattering in the house of the Lord, that the apostle was addressing careless or contentious talking that was causing distraction and confusion in the public assembly. Others feel that Paul could have been referring to uncontrolled ecstatic outcries by new converts that had been carried over from their previous pagan worship. At any rate, the Corinthian women *were* allowed to minister under proper leadership, but some had evidently carried their liberty too far.

Some scholars believe that the men sat on one side of the place of meeting and the women on the other. Interestingly, the separation of the sexes was historically founded in the Jewish temple, symbolized by the different courts, such as the Court of the Women or the Court of the Gentiles (which did not exist in Solomon's or Zerubbabel's temples). Herod's rebuilt temple was totally segregated, based upon the flimsy Rabbinical interpretation of Zechariah 12:12. Perhaps the women were calling out to their husbands across the room during the services. In that day, many women were not educated, so they appealed to their spouses who were. Also, teaching sessions often used the then popular question-and-answer format. At times there were heated debates. The main point is this: Paul wanted more than quiet women; he wanted submissive students of the Word, both men and women, who would learn without interruption.

There is one more thought-provoking view regarding this section of Paul's writings. Man is a trichotomy: spirit, soul, and body. The gender of the spirit realm is masculine; the gender of the soul is feminine. As the man is to be the head (source) of the woman, so the spirit is head over the soul. As has been noted, spirit is being and soul is expression. The soul of man (male or female) is his intellect, emotions, and will—what he thinks, feels, and wants. Soul is mind, human reasoning, carnal wisdom. May this "woman" ever be silent in our churches— the "woman" between our ears!

Let our souls (our soulish minds and those who speak from mere human reason, the words that come from our minds) keep silence in the churches. They should not be permitted to speak. If such will learn, let them ask the spirit, for it is a shame for the soul to speak in the church!

But I Suffer Not a Woman to Teach

Before we examine First Timothy 2:11-12, I want to stress again that women need to be under the covering of real spiritual authority (their husbands and their pastor)— so must the men.

There is a difference between being *under* a covering and *over* a man. It is first a difference in *attitude*, and then in *action*. Some women seek to subtly manipulate and cunningly control the man, to dominate him, and to work her own way. Such mannerisms are overbearing, insistent, maneuvering. The sharing of the Scriptures and prophetic utterances of a woman with these attitudes will often be abrasive, harsh, demanding, intruding, not an expression of a quiet and gentle spirit.

Paul noted in First Timothy 2:9-10 that women under spiritual authority will dress becomingly or modestly, adorning themselves with good deeds. They will be instructed in this area by the Holy Ghost, the spirit of sonship, the Child Trainer, not by the dictates of humanistic standards of holiness. Paul did not want the women to put their confidence in clothes. These Ephesian women whom Timothy was shepherding were following the then current fad of dressing like the goddess Diana, who had her skirt tucked up around her waist. Nudity and sexuality had been the previous forms of worship for many of these new converts, and they needed much practical instruction.

Moreover, the Greek word for "adorn" used in First Timothy 2:9 is *kosmeo* (compare with the English *cosmetic*) which means "to put in proper order; decorate; arrange." A similar word *kosmeo*, is translated as "modest" apparel and "good behavior" in First Timothy 2:9 and 3:2. The decorum of the Christian woman should reflect one of order. Her inward and outward appearance is to be in agreement with who she is as the King's daughter. Spiritual women are clothed with an internal nature, the character concealed in the heart, the imperishable quality of a quiet and gentle spirit that is of great value in the sight of God. The spiritual covering of a daughter of the King is her touchstone of grace, causing the glory of God to tabernacle on her.

Again, there are only two limitations to the woman's vast public ministry: In learning (receiving), she is to be quiet; in ministering (giving), she is to be covered. We have examined the covering of a spiritual woman, so now let's look at our second passage found in Paul's first letter to his spiritual son Timothy:

1 Tim. 2:11-12, KJV

Let the woman learn in silence with all subjection.

But I suffer not a woman to teach, nor to usurp authority over the man, but to be in silence.

This is the strongest Pauline statement used by men to keep women out of the pulpit and in the pew. Yet many Christian meetings were held in the houses of women— Chloe, Lydia, Mark's mother, Nympha, Priscilla, and others. Are we to presume that these hostesses were obliged to regress into absolute silence during meetings in their own homes?

Remember, the apostle is addressing women who are married, emphasizing the basic requirement of all ministry to reflect the divine order of the home and family. He uses the same word for "learn," meaning to "learn as a disciple," as he did in the Corinthian passage. The women of this time were uneducated and probably difficult to teach, for both Jews and Greeks considered female ignorance to be a virtue. To them Paul brought a revolutionary opportunity, vindicating them from the bondage of simple-mindedness, when he said, "Let the woman learn...!"

The wife is to learn in "silence," a different word that brings added insight. It means "stillness, desistance from hustle or language." Its root means "to keep one's seat (sedentary), to be undisturbed and undisturbing." The godly woman is marked by a quietness and tranquility that arises from within, causing no disturbance to others— a peaceable woman. As previously noted, "subjection" is derived from the root word translated as "under obedience" in the Corinthian passage.

Paul was reiterating that married Christian women, while learning, are to be quiet, under authority to their husbands. He wasn't arguing for their illiteracy as did the rabbis, nor did he put them down as silly, gossipy females. He encouraged them to learn.

"But I suffer not a woman to teach, nor to usurp authority over the man...." We must all be careful and honest when approaching this powerful but difficult passage. If it is used correctly, it can be a mighty, liberating force; if mishandled, it becomes a horrible, binding power.

The word for "man" used here is *aner* and it is singular. It does not refer to just any man or all "men." In this passage Paul is specifically referring the Christian woman to her own "man," her *husband*!

In our first passage, Paul did not "permit" or "allow" the women to speak while learning. Here the apostle adds that he does not "suffer" (the same word) women to "teach" or "give instruction" in the same setting. She is not to "usurp authority" over her husband; rather she is to dialogue with him at home. This rare word, *authenteo*, means "to act of oneself, to dominate; to exercise authority on one's own account, to domineer over; to thrust oneself." In its early Greek usage it referred to one who killed others or himself; its usage also carried sexual overtones. *Authenteo* later came to denote one who acted on his own authority. It can mean self-directed domination, gaining power through violence or sex.

Paul was essentially saying, "I do not allow a woman to teach that she can have dominion over her husband or control him, but women should be peaceable in the home." This underscores the spirit and action of genuine meekness.

Furthermore, there were Gnostics at Ephesus who enticed their male students with sexual overtures. Such groups accepted sexual license as Christian behavior. That city was renowned for the shrine of Diana and its thousands of temple prostitutes. This application of

Paul's words warn that he would not permit a woman to teach men by using female wiles, or to use her sexual advantage against her husband to get her own way.

Moreover, we must understand the historical and cultural backdrop of First Timothy; these Scriptures may have had merely a local or even temporary application. Accordingly, the passages that *seem* to restrict women can be confined to those to whom the letters are addressed—the new Christians living in pagan Corinth and Ephesus. Gnostic heresy was rampant in these cities, setting forth the belief that the female was a deformed male, even prohibiting physical contact with women. Greek and Egyptian influences embedded heathen practices within Christian services. Therefore converted Gentiles had to learn correct behavior because their culture was one of great festivity. Morality standards were diverse, and prostitution was a hallowed institution. Excessive perversion existed in their non-Christian world and lifestyle as a form of worship. Extremes in cross dressing, ecstatic worship, clamor, and hallucination had been their norm.

Paul's dressing restrictions may have had two motivations: one, to control the excessive pagan style; two, to conceal the Christians from the enemy. This Epistle was written about three years after the outbreak of persecution against the Christian Church by the infamous and barbarous Emperor Nero. This madman who butchered thousands of Christians had married a Jewess—the Christian women were free, the Jewish women were not. With the advent of Christianity, women were raised to the same level of equality as men, so Christians could be recognized by the actions of their women.

Paul wanted Christian women to pray and worship but not call attention to themselves. He did not want them to dress or act in a manner that would cause them to be conspicuous. He wisely asked them to keep a low profile, because their lives depended on it! Girl-watching Roman soldiers were looking for believers, so they eyed the women. For Christian women to be overly aggressive *in that day* would have jeopardized their families and the whole Christian community.

However, in the catacombs, where believers were living and worshiping, women were actively involved in the services. Recall that on some of these walls have been found etchings and paintings depicting women preaching and serving Communion. The phrase, "I suffer not a woman to teach..." appears to be timeless. But the verb in the Greek text is present, active indicative and thus reads, "I am *not presently* permitting a woman to teach...." Nero is dead. Go ahead and minister, ladies!

Having noted that the gender of the spirit is masculine and the gender of the soul is feminine, Paul was also saying, "Let the soul learn in silence with all subjection, for I do not allow the soul realm to teach, or to usurp authority over the spirit realm, but to be in silence!" Sadly, those who have taken the words of Paul out of context to substantiate their man-made traditions and put down the public ministry of women have done that very thing!

Finally, First Timothy 2:13-15 needs to be addressed. It would appear that Paul is blaming women for everything.

1 Tim. 2:13, KJV

For Adam was first formed, then Eve.

Here Paul is using the example of Adam and Eve to underscore domestic order. We have already learned that Adam and Eve were one in the beginning. Adam was created "first" in time. They were both "formed" or "molded or shaped"; this word was also used of artists who wrought in clay or wax.

1 Tim. 2:14, KJV

And Adam was not deceived, but the woman being deceived was in the transgression.

Indeed, Eve was "deceived." This word means "cheated, deluded, beguiled." But Adam knowingly walked into the transgression with his eyes wide open— that was worse! He was "with her" in the temptation. The serpent tempted the man *and* the woman. "Ye" and "your" are plural pronouns in the Book of Genesis. The results of the fall happened to "both" of them at the same time, as recorded in Genesis 3:4-7. To blame Eve for the fall and to attribute the subsequent consequences to her deception is to foster hostility and a prejudice that she can never live down.

Some feel that Adam knew the name or the nature of the serpent; Eve did not. Accordingly, the woman was not "dumber" than Adam; she was just newer in the time of her creation, and thus more vulnerable. Adam sinned with understanding. His was a conscious choice based upon knowledge. Adam failed to teach his wife; therefore, Paul might have been admonishing the brothers not to make the same mistake.

Adam was beside Eve, and *they* were without excuse. Eve should have protected herself and taken dominion, and so should have Adam. Eve was tricked and deceived into believing the devil. Adam watched her but did not intervene; then he did the same thing deliberately.

Moreover, deception takes place in the realm of the soul—the "woman." Men who do not know or proclaim the whole counsel have used Paul's words to put down the woman. These men need to read Romans 5:12-21 again! Adam and Eve *both* sinned—they were in it together. God called *their* name Adam, and both male man and female man were driven from the garden.

1 Tim. 2:15, KJV

Notwithstanding she shall be saved in childbearing....

Women are not saved by childbearing because not all women have children, not all births are painful, and not all women are married. Although this verse is a promise to women with regard to birthing children, there is more to it. The woman will be saved "in" childbearing. This is the preposition *dia*, a primary preposition denoting the channel or instrumentality of an act. "Childbearing" is the Greek word *teknogonia*, a compound of two words— *teknon*, which means "child," and *gennao*, which means "to beget, to birth." The Amplified Bible catches the original meaning, "...through the Childbearing or by the birth of the divine Child." Paul declared in Galatians 4:4 that God "sent forth His Son, made of a woman...."

Gen. 3:15, NIV

And I will put enmity between you and the woman, and between your offspring and hers; He will crush your head, and you will strike His heel.

Eve, the woman, would be saved through the Child that she would bear—the Seed of the woman who would bruise the serpent's head! This is the Emancipation Proclamation of women, their Magna Carta. God gave the mother of all living a special promise, "Eve, you will bring forth a Savior. You shall bear a Child, and He will bring salvation!" Jesus, the divine Child, was born of a woman and became our Savior, forever liberating women from the tyranny of religious ignorance and superstition!

Women can pray, proclaim, and learn. They are no longer under the shadow of Eve's deception any more than men are under the shadow of Adam's willful sin. Jesus redeemed the woman and the man from the curse.

Jesus, the chief Apostle, and Paul, the literary apostle who wrote half the New Testament, were not prejudiced against women. Jesus Christ closed the door to the Old Covenant and ushered in a New Covenant wherein there is neither male nor female— only oneness in Christ. He set the captives (men and women) free from all the bondages of sin, the curse, and religion. Paul was often accused of disturbing social order and changing age-old customs as he brought emancipation to women.

Did Jesus say that women cannot teach? Did the apostles? Does the Bible? No! Then who did? The Judaizers declared this, relying upon their oral law! Should women remain bound because of Christian traditions that are based upon human interpretations? No more than the women serving under Jesus' ministry remained bound to their Jewish traditions. Nowhere does the Bible forbid any woman from serving God in any capacity to which He calls and prepares her.

In these epochal days of great outpourings of the Holy Spirit, we must remember that Joel 2:28-29 provides the clearest biblical definition of real revival: It must include the daughters with the sons, and the handmaids with the servants!

Let me close this chapter with the challenging words of a great scholar and champion of the right for women to minister:

"And what will the women of our day do?...We cannot escape; we must either choose the best that could be, from the highest standpoint, or by failing to choose prove ourselves Esaus. God has given us the challenge to our faith. Shall we despise our birthright? God forbid!"[1]

In Christ, there is neither male nor female. Come out of the law and into Christ. Come out of obedience and into union—men and woman walking together as one with the will of the Father. All sexist prejudice crumbles at the foot of the cross. Paul boldly proclaimed to the Corinthians that he would know nothing and no one except Jesus Christ and Him crucified. May every person say, "I refuse to know you as male or female—I will only know you through the cross!"

> "Jesus took a towel and washed the disciples' feet. When His disciples asked about their ranking in the coming Kingdom, Jesus reminded them that Gentiles sought power and status. Christians— both male and female— should, like the Son of Man, come to serve, not to be served. Questions about authority in the church, and particularly about the ministry of women, might be resolved more biblically if attention were given to the fact that 'ministry' means 'serving.' "[2]

Jesus came to deliver us from sexual prejudice. He loves men and woman, boys and girls. Our King is also color-blind. He has not lifted one natural people group above any other in His sight. In fact, He is now calling out a divine Race from among the races.

Part Three

Race

"And hath made of one blood all nations of men...."

Acts 17:26

Foreword by Bishop Earl P. Paulk

I would like to commend Kelley Varner on being led by the Spirit and doing the necessary research to write *The Three Prejudices*. He has gone through the Scriptures with a fine-toothed comb, establishing the biblical foundation for racial harmony. I am impressed with such an eloquent work.

I am more impressed with the conviction that the message of this book is vitally important for this day. We must lay aside our prejudices, whether they are based on gender, race, or nationality. When Jesus prayed for unity in John 17, He had something far more in mind than just a casual knowledge or acquaintance among ourselves. The time has come that we must strive with determination to bring forth real unity.

It is commonly known that I pastor a church that includes thousands of black people, and that I have worked diligently for years to bring harmony between races. Books like this are a positive response to this need, offered with a spirit of sacrifice like that of Dr. Martin Luther King, Jr.

It is imperative that this thrust does not cease. To do so would be to set the stage for great bloodshed in our nation.

Take time to read and re-read these chapters on racial prejudice. They will answer many of your biblical questions and give you a firm foundation from which to proclaim the gospel of the Kingdom and true unity in Christ.

Chapter Seven

Ham Was Not Cursed

"And God blessed Noah and his sons...."

Genesis 9:1

Christ is not prejudiced. His Spirit rises above all bigotry. He is not a sexist, nor a racist. Jesus loves men and women, and He died for all. Our God is a global God who loves all people.

Racism, the notion that one's own ethnic stock or skin color is superior to another, is the second of the three prejudices.

Racism is the mother of bigotry. It is exampled in the twentieth century by "Jim Crowism" (discrimination against people of color by "legal" means or sanctions), Nazism and Neo-Nazism, the skinheads, the KKK (Ku Klux Klan) and other white supremacy movements, anti-Semitism, and apartheid. All these belief systems spring from a haughty attitude of racial superiority.

Unfortunately, racism does not end with these social and political groups. It has also contaminated our churches. I've met many preachers who know something about the Kingdom, yet remain biased and opinionated when it comes to race. I've heard them crack their jokes. God will hold these persons accountable for their words! Without first overcoming their racial prejudice, these preachers will never sit and reign with the King in His throne.

Racism is hereditary, environmental, and reactionary.

Hereditary racism is passed down from parent to child, from one generation to the next—usually during the first five years of a child's life. Thus the lie of racism is inherited. Parents on both sides of the issue are actively teaching (mostly by example) their children racism under the guise of religious training. Unfortunately, much of this kind of racism is fostered by our churches. God is not pleased with "white" churches or "black" churches; these are less significant adjectives subordinating a more important noun.

Environmental racism consists of racial attitudes, beliefs, and erroneous concepts of ethnic superiority caused by the overpowering influence of one's environment and associations. Beware of hate groups and racist organizations (including some "churches"). Many are confusing redemptive rights with human rights.

Reactionary or reverse racism is triggered in a suppressed minority by ill treatment and acts of racism inflicted on them by others. There is an alarming rise of this in America, as indicated by the "Nation of Islam" and other groups.

God hates racism in any form—it is sin. Racism is rooted in degeneracy, pride, superior attitudes, ignorance, and fear. Unregenerate Adamic flesh is the soil from which racism springs. Included here are pride of place (social status), pride of face (physical attributes), pride of grace (religious or denominational traditions), and pride of race (based on skin color or ethnicity).

Men exaggerate their own importance to overshadow the value of others who are different. Everyone in the United States (with the exception of native Americans) has descended from relatives who sailed across the water to get here. People of color are not the only ones who got "off the boat," although they were the only ones forced "on the boat." Stereotyped ignorance is the result of the absence of knowledge, wisdom, or understanding. Men have failed to study God's Word for enlightenment. This has fostered many absurd concepts and doctrines of demons.

Men fear what they do not know. They are often afraid to fellowship with those of another race, apprehensive of what it might produce in other areas of life. Most people simply fear change. Fear that isolates and separates men from one another thrives upon complacency. It is easier to flow with the crowd.

One Blood

"Red and yellow, black and white, they are precious in His sight...."

God does see skin color. He's not naive. He created skin color! But those who believe that different races should not be in the same congregation on earth will be shocked in Heaven. Doctor Luke declared in Acts 17:26-27 that God has "made of one blood all nations of men for to dwell on all the face of the earth, and hath determined the times before appointed, and the bounds of their habitation; that they should seek the Lord...."

All "nations" came from one blood. This is the Greek word *ethnos* (English "ethnic") and means "a race," and denotes a nation or people. All "races" have one beginning. The billions of people who call the earth their home all came from one source of blood—Adam and Eve, the father and mother of all mankind. That *one blood* was preserved in the deluge through the three sons of Noah. Nowhere in Genesis 10, the table of 70 nations—26 from Shem, 30 from Ham, and 14 from Japheth—is there any mention of skin color. God wants men and women to seek Him, regardless of color, race, or tribe!

All these nations were genetically founded in the three sons of Noah. Shem was the father of the Semitic nations— the Jews, the Arabs, the Syrians, the Assyrians, the Babylonians, and the Persians. From Ham descended the Egyptians, the Phoenicians, the Hittites and other Canaanites, the Africans, the Mongols and the Chinese, the Japanese, the American Indians, the Eskimos, the South Sea islanders, and many others. The Japhetic nations include the Indo-Europeans or Caucasians, the Russians, the Medes, the Germans, the Arameans, the Turks, and the Greeks.

Yet as recently as World War II, an injured white man would not be given a direct transfusion from an Asian, black man, or red man because of fear (ignorance). Medical science has since discovered that apart from different blood types, all blood is the *same* unless it is diseased. It doesn't matter what color you are, what generation you were born in, what language you speak, or what level of education you've received: we all came from *one blood*! Mankind has one Father God who created us all, so let us deal with one another justly and mercifully.

In the Book of Genesis, God separated (not divided) the peoples by language, family, and nation—not by race. For God, color is never a basis for separation, division, or segregation (in America, South Africa, or anywhere else).

Luke declared in Acts 17:26 that God has given to every man, race, and nation a designated time and certain habitable boundaries. There was and is a divine appointment, an established time of world leadership for all three of Noah's sons—Shem, Ham, and Japheth.

Today is not the day of the black man (who descended from Ham)—he had his day for 2,000 years (as exampled by the Egyptians). The Jews who came from Shem had their day for 2,000 years, ending in the days of Jesus and the first apostles. The white man, the Indo-European nations, the sons of Japheth, are near the end of their allotted time of dominion. Mankind has labored for six days, six thousand years (Ex. 20:9-11; 2 Pet. 3:8); now it is time for the Lord to have *His* day! It is time for Christ to reign! Today is the day for His Church!

Predestination certainly applies to spiritual things. But divine determination also applies to natural things, such as gender and race. Jeremiah 13:23 asks, "Can [would] the Ethiopian change his skin or the leopard its spots? Neither can you do good who are accustomed to doing evil" (NIV). Paul echoed in Romans 9:20b, "Shall the thing formed say to him that formed it, Why hast thou made me thus?"

It should be clear that one's ethnicity or gender was a definite act of God and not a blind chance or mistake. He chose to make you the color you are, and He gave you the features you have (Ps. 139:14). Never allow anyone's irrational racist remarks make you feel inferior, insulted, or ugly. You are beautiful and acceptable in His sight, so the opinions and words of others do not matter. Mindsets of inferiority created by generations of discrimination are difficult to change. Learn to accept the ethnicity and personal characteristics of others without partiality or bias. To have respect of persons is sin.

It is the view of some that the peoples of the earth have experienced physiological changes directly related to their geographical, environmental, and dietary peculiarities. It is briefly mentioned here for your consideration. Accordingly, God knew that man would overspread the earth and thus made him environmentally adaptable.

The Shulamite woman in Song of Solomon 1:5-6 declared, "I am black, but comely, O ye daughters of Jerusalem, as the tents of Kedar, as the curtains of Solomon. Look not upon me, because I am black, because the sun hath looked upon me...." The New King James Version says, "...I am dark, because the sun has tanned me..." (Song 1:6).

The true skin (or the true man) cannot be seen with the natural eye. We only see the covering that protects the true skin, which has nerve endings and minute blood vessels that otherwise would be damaged by the sun. This true skin is basically the same color in all men everywhere.

The outer layer of the skin that contains pigment is the epidermis; it has five layers for the primary purpose of protection. As its surface is worn away, new cells are supplied. Although there is no pigment-reproducing chemical in the true skin, the dermis, there is such a chemical substance stored in the epidermis, hair, and eyes: melanin. Melanin is released in the epidermis in amounts necessary to shield the dermis from the sun. This produces a richer color to the skin so that ultra-violet rays cannot penetrate—thus the body "tans" itself. Color is not race. Skin color has nothing to do with the image of God.

In Caucasians melanin is found only in the three deepest epidermal layers. In blacks, it is found in all five layers. The uppermost layer of the skin contains another pigment called carotene. Together with melanin, it produces the yellow color of the skin in some races. The pink color of Caucasian skin is due to blood vessels in the dermis that are not heavily masked by pigment. Furthermore, in all races there are areas of the human body that do not totally mask the color of true skin—the fingernails, toenails, the palms, and the soles of the feet. Color comes from the effects of the sun. The epidermis is no more than protective clothing, and clothing comes in all colors.[1]

Ham Was Blessed By God, Not Cursed

Prejudiced men have used a story from the first book of the Bible in their attempts to scripturally substantiate racial prejudice. They have claimed that their prejudice is justified because of a curse God placed upon Ham.

However, God blessed Noah and his three sons, *including Ham*! The account is found in Genesis 9:18-28.

For almost four centuries men have debated what actually took place in Noah's tent. Some say that Ham took advantage of his drunken father and had a homosexual relationship with him. Others feel that Ham enjoyed observing his father's nudity and made jokes about it to Shem and Japheth. From these kinds of allegations men have asserted that Ham was responsible for the perpetual enslavement of his descendants, and that these descendants were subsequently cursed with black skin—the infamous "curse of Ham."

This religious tradition teaches that blacks were cursed, and made inferior and subservient to whites. Such uninformed ignorance has mentally and emotionally scarred many young hearts, often sparking an anger toward God because of these religious traditions ("Mommy, why did God do this to me?"). Men have deceitfully distorted, misinterpreted, and misused the Word of God to promote racism and other doctrines of devils.

Passionate white supremacists twist God's Word as a weapon to justify their bigotry. Angry black activists have retaliated by misquoting God's Word to justify the same kind of hatred toward whites. Many Protestant preachers in America, the Caribbean, and in countries across the world have taught their congregations that Noah's curse was leveled at the black man. As "proof" they point to his black skin and the lowly position that blacks have held for hundreds of years in Western society, saying, "Those people were created to serve others. It's God's will."

Bigoted men have concluded that Ham and his black descendants were cursed, and that the black color of their skin was the penalty. White, Bible-believing Christians started this ungodly theory and introduced it to the rest of society. This narrow-mindedness has influenced Christian writings (commentaries and Bible dictionaries) and even some major encyclopedias. Tragically, it was the Church that gave this awful tradition to the world. Although it's all right for a white man to repent for historical and contemporary sins of racial injustice or a black man to regret his bitterness (which is unfulfilled vengeance), the Church also needs to apologize.

Men have used Genesis 9:18-28 to religiously justify and underpin the historical evil of slavery, later allowing city, state, and federal government laws to permit separate restrooms, restaurants, schools, health care facilities, drinking fountains, and cemeteries.

The heresy of British Israelism, or Anglo-Saxonism, goes even further, declaring that only the white race is the true Israel of God, connecting the United States and Great Britain with the ancient tribes of Ephraim and Manasseh. Extremes of this unscriptural view (which presumes a natural line of descent that defies all known history, anthropology, and reasonable genetic research) have outrageously called people of color "the beasts of the field"—without a soul, outside the Adamic realm.

What sheer idiocy! This so-called "Identity" message appeals to the soulish intellect of men under the guise of revelation knowledge. This middle-of-the-road position bears the fruit of exclusivism. It is a feeble attempt to sew up the veil that Jesus rent. If I were God, I'd bring a great revival through the Blacks of this country and the Third World nations of the earth. To these ministries I proclaim, "Rise up, brethren! Let nothing or no one spoil you through philosophy and vain deceit!"

Was Ham cursed? In Genesis 9:1, God didn't curse anyone! He actually blessed Ham, the second son of Noah. It was Noah (awaking from a drunken stupor) who cursed Canaan, not Ham, in Genesis 9:25. Ham did enter his father's tent, but he did no wrong. Ham's descendants (with the exception of Canaan) were not cursed, and no one's skin was turned black.

The curse placed upon Canaan had nothing to do with the black race! Noah's curse centered exclusively upon Canaan's descendants, and it was historically fulfilled from a Semitic (Shem's) perspective when Abraham defeated certain Canaanitish tribes in Genesis 14 and when Joshua and the children of Israel conquered and subdued all the *Canaanite nations* in the land of promise (see Gen. 10:15-18; 15:18-21; Ex. 3:8; 15:15-16; Josh. 9:23-27; Judg. 1:28; 1 Kings 9:20-21)!

"Ham" appears 17 times in the Bible and not one mention of a curse is to be found (see Gen. 5:32; 6:10; 7:13; 10:1). "Ham" is taken from the Hebrew *Cham*, which means "hot (from the tropical habitat); Cham, a son of Noah; also (as a patronymic) his descendants or their country." "Ham" has been translated to mean "black, sun-hot, hot or dark, man with dark skin, colored, swarthy."

Ham was black; Shem and Japheth were brown. They lived in a warm climate, and it hadn't rained in Ham's lifetime—most of the 120 years Noah was preaching. Consider the diet of Noah and his family and the effects of a century of constant sunlight. Ham had been black for 100 years when this incident happened. He was born black, the way God made him.

From Ham came a broad definition of the black race, which includes people whose skin tones range from very light to very dark and whose hair textures range from coarse to very straight. Ham and the other sons of Noah had been told stories by their grandfather Lamech about the beginning of time. The Garden of Eden had rich, dark reddish-brown soil—from which Adam was made. Eden also included Ethiopia which means "the land of black people." In other words, the first man, Adam, had dark skin.

The record of Genesis 6:10-20 shows that from Ham came great countries and civilizations: Egypt (called "Ham" in Psalms 78:51; 105:23,27; 106:22), Ethiopia, Babylon, and great cities like Nineveh, none of which were cursed for what took place in Noah's tent.

Genesis 10:6 identifies the sons of Ham as Cush, Mizraim, Phut, and Canaan. The tribe of Mizraim settled in Egypt, while the tribes of Cush (Ethiopia) and Phut (Libya) settled in other parts of Africa. The tribe of Canaan populated Phoenicia and Palestine.

Cush is Ethiopia: Both names mean "black." The term "Ethiopia" evolved from the Greek words *ethios* ("burned") and *opes* ("face")— *ethiosopes* means "burned face." Caanan was cursed, not Cush, the one from whom many feel that the black race descended. Cush was not cursed!

The truth of what actually happened that day in Noah's tent will be discovered through the writings of Moses gleaned from the information he learned from Jethro, his black father-in-law (a relative of Midian, son of Keturah, Abraham's Canaanite wife). Having been raised by Pharaoh's daughter, Moses knew no father figure until he met Jethro.

Ham was the only eyewitness to the events of our story. He *saw* something in Genesis 9:22. The Bible does not say that he *did* anything. Some feel that this word for "saw" indicates an evil, lustful looking. But there is a better explanation.

Noah had gotten drunk on his own success. He had begun farming and started a vineyard—the very thing that he planted and reaped was the thing that caused his downfall! Noah got himself drunk. We are not told if his wife was also drunk. Nonetheless, it was Canaan, not Ham, who took advantage of this situation.

Ham was the second, not the youngest son of Noah. The term "younger son" in Genesis 9:24 was a Hebraic idiom for "the smallest son," and is highly likely that it was an expression for *grandson.*[2] Again, it was *Canaan*, not Ham, who was cursed. Noah, not God, was the one who cursed his grandson as a result of what he discovered upon awaking from his drunken state. In this chapter God blessed; man cursed.

The key to unlocking this passage is the biblical meaning of Ham seeing "the nakedness of his father." This word for "nakedness" in Genesis 9:22 means "nudity;

figuratively, disgrace," and is translated in the King
James Version as "shame, uncleanness." It has also been
rendered as "indecent thing; impoverishment, dishonor,
a feeling of vulnerableness, filthiness, the uncovering of
which is for licentious or lewd purposes." This term in-
volves more than mere looking. Something sinful was
going on in that tent, and it involved Canaan. However,
in the light of Jesus' definition of adultery (Mt. 5:28), it is
possible that Canaan's involvement was limited to
watching.

Canaan did not sin because he saw grandfather Noah
without clothes on. It was common for fathers and sons
to bathe together in the river. Nudity had nothing to do
with it. Noah was 500 years old when he began to have
children and 600 when he went into the ark. These boys
had seen their papa naked plenty of times. Yet the scriptural account states that Ham saw his father's "nakedness" and that Shem and Japheth covered their father's
"nakedness" (Gen. 9:22-23). What is the meaning of a
"father's nakedness"?[3] In addition to this passage in
Genesis, this phrase is found only two other times in the
Bible, written by Moses in the priestly Book of Leviticus:

Lev. 18:8, KJV

*The nakedness of thy father's **wife** shalt thou not
uncover: it is thy father's nakedness.*

Lev. 20:11, KJV

*And the man that lieth with his father's **wife** hath
uncovered his father's nakedness: both of them shall
surely be put to death; their blood shall be upon them.*

The term "father's nakedness" had to do with sexual intercourse. Compare the word "knew," or the phrase "went in unto" (Gen. 4:1; 16:4). Moses talked about this "nakedness" elsewhere in the law (Lev. 20:17-21). Canaan did not desire to have sex with grandfather Noah, but with his grandmother. And he was cursed for it!

When Ham happened upon this perversion, he went into the tent (as would any good father) and dragged out his son Canaan. The Levitical economy later judged this kind of sin with the death penalty. As Ham was dealing with his son, he called for his brothers to go in and cover their mother, which they did.

Noah's nakedness ("his father's nakedness") was the uncovering of his wife. Paul declared in Ephesians 5:28 that men ought "...to love their wives as their own bodies. He that loveth his wife loveth himself." For Canaan to violate Noah's wife was to violate Noah.

Compare similar incidences. Lot's daughters got him drunk and violated him; Jacob's firstborn son Reuben violated Jacob's concubine Bilhah (Gen. 19:30-38; 35:22). Lot wasn't cursed for his daughters' sexual sins. Jacob wasn't cursed for Reuben's promiscuity. Jesse wasn't cursed for David's sin with Bathsheba, nor was Ham cursed when Canaan violated his grandmother.

Prejudice is ignorance of the truth, and God's Word is truth. Prejudice is pre-judging without having all the necessary information. Simple Bible exegesis and the comparing of Scripture with Scripture tells us what the Bible *says* and therefore what it *means*! But most folks do not think in biblical terms because they do not read the Bible.

Ironically, in those biblical incidences where a curse involved skin color, God turned the skin *white*, not black! Miriam and Gehazi were smitten with leprosy and became "white as snow" (Num. 12:10; 2 Kings 5:27). Miriam was upset with her little brother's black wife. God responded, "If you want to see white, I'll show you white!"

There is *no* curse upon the black race! If there were (but there is not), Jesus' finished work in His death and resurrection would have reversed it (Gal. 3:10-14; Eph. 4:8-10)! To all people of color, I declare, "You cannot be cursed and blessed at the same time! Make up your mind and receive the truth of God's Word!"

There is no person or nation that is locked into a curse. The leaves of the tree of life in Revelation 22 are for the healing of the nations— *all* of them. Indeed, the multi-colored leaves of that Tree called Christ could well *be* all the races of the earth.[4]

If there is a curse upon mankind today, where is it? The Bible says in Proverbs 3:33, "The curse of the Lord is in the house of the wicked: but He blesseth the habitation of the just." Paul added in Romans 6:23, "For the wages of sin is death...."

Adam, without God, is cursed. Holiness has nothing to do with the color of one's skin, birthplace, nation, or background. The curse now is upon the house of the wicked. It has to do with sin, not skin. Skin color should never be used as the basis of discrimination; nor should it become the excuse for non-productivity by those who feel victimized.

No curse is permanent! If that were true, none of us would be here. We couldn't sing, "I'm a new creation, I'm a brand-new man, old things have passed away, I've been born again...."

My Christian friend, first and foremost, you are not a black man, or a white man, or a red man, or a yellow man—you are one with Him who is the God-man! Born of the Spirit, you are spirit. Mankind is of one blood. Skin color has nothing to do with the image of God. God is colorless, or contains all color (as all things are made by Him). The image of God has everything to do with spirit—the unveiled face (heart) has been stripped of racism. To God, there is only one ethnic group—His children, His Church.[5]

Circumcision or uncircumcision, black or white, avails nothing; it has no strength or force. The only thing that counts with God is the new creation. Rejoice! Jesus Christ has set men of every color free! The only way to join the races and the nations into one, holy spiritual Race is to bring them into Christ; they will be made one in Him.

Ham was not cursed. Ham and his descendants were blessed, as abundantly evidenced by their anointed presence in biblical and world history.

Chapter Eight

People of Color in the Bible and History

"…Ethiopia shall soon stretch
out her hands unto God."

Psalm 68:31

Ham was blessed, not cursed. Yet since the opening years of the sixteenth century, much Christian biblical scholarship has been the close ally of racism, often deliberately and at times unconsciously. This unholy alliance has run the gamut from the avid support of the black inferiority myth to a mere indifference to the situation. In all likelihood there are many Christians today who still believe that the so-called "curse of Ham" fell upon the black man. This fallacy was once taught by leading educators of their day, and the successors of those scholars and writers have done very little to erase the fallacy.

Secular writers have done more to correct these fabrications than their biblical colleagues. This is why many young black Americans call the holy Scriptures "the white man's Bible."[1] Bitter religious voices tell people of color that they cannot serve the God of the Bible because it is geared to benefit the white man and suppress the black man. But *all* men are hopeless apart from the power of His living Word.

The contemporary issue is that many Black Muslims teach that Islam is the natural religion of the black man and Christianity is the religion of the Europeans. History does support some of the questions that the black follow-ers of Islam raise, so they think that their extreme claims are justified. One U.S. Supreme Court case in particular, the "Dred Scott" controversy in 1857, expressed the pre-vailing opinion in America at the time that the black man was indeed inferior to the white man. That ungodly ju-dicial decision gave white Americans the legal "right" to treat blacks as second-class slaves and shamelessly al-lowed our nation to document racism in its highest court.

The architect of the Black Muslim faith in America was a black man named Elijah Muhammed. Born in San-dersville, Georgia, he knew firsthand the injustice of ra-cism. This man was born Elijah Poole, the son of a Baptist preacher. But he was later converted to a black American version of Islam in the 1930s by W.D. Farad (or Fard). Their forerunner, born in 1866, was Timothy Drew (later Noble Drew Ali) who established a school in Newark, New Jersey, to promote his understanding of Islam. The present-day voice for the Nation of Islam is Louis Abdul Farrakhan (or Farrakan). Unfortunately, thousands of blacks have been converted to this hateful way of thinking, including prominent black entertainers, athletes, and educators. The great black historian, Dr. W.E.B. DuBois, addressed this historical question with regard to Islam and Christianity.

Dubois noted that the cross preceded the crescent (a symbol of Islam) in some of the remotest parts of Africa. He notes that Christ was born in the first century, Muhammed in the seventh. The Judeo-Christian Bible is older than the Qur'an. Blacks in Ethiopia were students of the Scriptures and had built churches on African soil before Muhammed was ever born. The spread of Islam was political and economic as much as it was spiritual (as a result of the Arabic conquest).

Most shockingly, Arab Muslims enslaved blacks long before Europeans adopted their awful practice! The Black Muslim movement in America was largely built on the premise that Moslems and Arabs were ethnically identified, friendly, respectful, and hospitable toward blacks. Christianity was ethnically identified with Europeans and considered a party to the system that sought to control and deny black people their human dignity and freedom. However, the spread of Islam among blacks was a result of Muslim military conquest. It was illegal for a true Moslem to hold another Moslem in slavery; many blacks in conquered lands "converted" to Islam to gain their freedom!

Others have documented that Christianity had reached West Africa prior to the period in which West Africans were brought to America as slaves. Islam is, therefore, not the natural religion of the black race. In Islam man is searching for God; in Christianity God came down in the person of His Son to search for man. In Islam men are saved by works; in Christianity men of all races are saved by faith.[2]

The Bible is for all men. Therefore it is important to see how powerful an influence men and women of color had on the people and events recorded in both testaments. Children and young people of color need positive role models.

This chapter is written to proclaim truth, not to exalt or promote flesh. Some have become obsessed with this subject, going beyond the written Word to push their own specific race or agenda. But real truth never exalts a people in terms of their flesh: Truth always brings glory to God.

The first man Adam was neither black nor white. He was made from dirt, which can be a variety of colors, either brown, black, dark, dusky, red, or sandy. He was probably reddish-brown, as his name indicates. It is interesting that a black Adam and Eve appeared on the cover of the January 11, 1988, issue of *Newsweek* magazine. As noted, Ethiopia, which means "black," was part of the garden of Eden. Also, the great Jewish historian Josephus and others have associated the Gihon River with the Nile; since according to the Septuagint, the word *Nile* is a Greek translation of the Hebrew word *Gihon*. Other clues point to Africa as the cradle of humanity because of its vast resources and the archaeologists' findings of the oldest bones and artifacts in West and East Africa. The Greeks called the Nile "the River of Ham."[3]

Noah (or his wife) had to have been a person of color in order to beget children of color (Gen. 9:18-19). It is genetically impossible for bright or fair-complexioned persons to produce dark-skinned children. Regardless, Adam and Eve, and later Noah and his wife, possessed the genetic makeup that produced the three basic races of mankind.

Cush, whose name means "black," was the father of Havilah, whose name was associated with a land near to the garden of Eden (Gen. 2:10-11; 10:7).

Cush was also the father of Nimrod, the first king in the earth to establish an empire. Nimrod was called a mighty hunter "before the Lord" (Gen. 10:6-10; 11:2). Of all the names listed in the genealogical table of Genesis 10, Nimrod stands alone in the biographical information given him. He became a pattern by which men measured strength, might, intellectual and military prowess, and knowledge of how to set up government. The beginning of his kingdom was in the land of Shinar, the starting point of civilization.

Caphtor, the seventh son of Mizraim, grandson of Ham, was the father of the black Philistines (Gen. 10:6, 13-14; Jer. 47:4; Amos 9:7).

The grandson of Ham and the firstborn of Canaan was Sidon (Gen. 10:15). Sidon and Tyre were the home bases for the powerful people (craftsmen, merchants, and navigators) known as the Zidonians or Phoenicians.

Canaan, Ham's son, begat the Jebusites. Melchizedek was King of Salem, or Jerusalem, a royal city occupied by Jebusites (Gen. 10:15-16; 14:18; 2 Sam. 5:26). Whoever this mysterious man was, he was a man of color.

Hagar, the dark-skinned Egyptian handmaid to Sarah, bore Ishmael, Abraham's son (Gen. 16:1-16).

Abraham had the majority of his children with Keturah (Gen. 25:1-3). Sheba and Dedan, Cushite names, were two of their grandchildren.

Asenath, the Egyptian wife of Joseph, has been traced back to the Hamitic line through Cush (Gen. 41:45).

Asenath bore Joseph two sons, Ephraim and Manasseh, also men of color (Gen. 41:50-52).

Moses married the Ethiopian woman Zipporah, daughter of Jethro, descendant of Midian (Ex. 2:15-21; Num. 12:1,10). When God's chosen leader was openly challenged and rebuked by Miriam and Aaron for his interracial marriage (perhaps they were jealous over the influence of Jethro in Moses' life), Jehovah came to his defense. God despises marriages and relationships with unsaved, idolatrous mates and companions. An unequal yoke in the eyes of God is for His children to become joined with unbelievers, not with un-whites or un-blacks.

Having been reared by a black princess, Pharaoh's daughter, Moses' first and only father figure was Jethro (whose name means "his excellence"), the priest of Midian, and a Kenite. Jethro mentored Moses, and then released him to deliver God's people (Ex. 4:18). Exodus 18 records that this great black leader imparted wise, administrative instruction concerning the governing of God's people.

Hobab, Zipporah's brother and Jethro's son, was asked to be the eyes of the people of God (Num. 10:29-31; Judg. 4:11). He was quite experienced with the wilderness. The prophet Isaiah declared that Ethiopia and Seba were Israel's "ransom" or "covering" (scouts) in the wilderness (Is. 43:1-3).

Joshua, Moses' successor, was of the tribe of Ephraim, who was the younger of two sons born to Joseph and his Egyptian wife Asenath (Gen. 41:50-52; Num. 13:8; 1 Chron. 7:22-27).

As noted, Salmon married the Canaanite Rahab, the ancestress of David and Jesus— she had Hamitic blood in her family, for the Canaanites were descendants of Canaan, one of the sons of Ham (Gen. 10:6; see also Mt. 1:4-6; Heb. 11:31; Jas. 2:23-25).

The great warrior Caleb (of the tribe of Judah) was a Kenezite, or Kenite, a faction of the Midianites. For Judah fathered twins, Pharez and Zarah, by a Hamitic woman named Tamar (see Gen. 15:19; 38; Num. 32:11-12; 1 Sam. 15:6).

Othniel, Caleb's younger brother, was the first judge of Israel (Judg. 3:7-11; 1 Chron. 4:13-15).

The heroine Jael was the wife of Heber the Kenite (Judg. 4:11,17).

In his day, Job was "the greatest of all the men of the east" (Job 1:3,8,14-15), and he was probably a man of color. The Sabeans (the people of Saba, or Seba, which is very close to Sheba in northern Ethiopia) attacked his possessions.

Goliath, the Philistine giant warrior slain by David, was a descendant of Ham. His lineage was from Mizraim, whose seed produced the Philistines (Gen. 10:6, 13-14; 1 Sam. 17).

Another example was the giant King Og, the Amorite ruler of Bashan in the days of Moses (Gen. 10:16; Num. 21:33-35; Deut. 3:1,11).

Arba was a giant Canaanite who produced the people known as the Anakims. These giants descended from Ham through Canaan (Num. 13:28-33; Deut. 9:1-3; Josh. 14:15).

There were other dark-skinned giant groups called Zamzummim or Zuzim, Emim, and Rephaim (Gen. 14:5; Deut. 2:10-11,20-21).[4]

Bathsheba, which means "daughter of Sheba," was black; Sheba was the grandson of Cush. Her first husband, Uriah the Hittite, son of Heth, a descendant of Ham, was also a man of color (see Gen. 10:6-7,15; 2 Sam. 11; Mt. 1:6).

Solomon was the son of David by Bathsheba (2 Sam. 12:24). The wisdom of this man who was at least half-black exceeded the wisdom of all the children of the "east country," and all the wisdom of Egypt (both regions populated by dark-skinned people). (See First Kings 4:30.)

As already noted, the Shulamite of the Song of Solomon (perhaps this was Abishag) was black (Song 1:5-6; 1 Kings 1–2).

Hiram, a black king of Tyre or Phoenicia, was a descendant of Canaan's first son, Zidon. His land was known for its professional craftsmen and commercial control over lumber in Lebanon. He is remembered for his architectural skill, which was displayed during a 20-year period of designing palaces and helping to build the temple of Solomon (see Gen. 10:15; 1 Kings 5:1; 11:1; 1 Chron. 22:4).

Cushi, a servant of David, was ordered by Captain Joab to run and notify the king concerning the death of prince Absalom (2 Sam. 18:21-32).

Ismaiah was a Gibeonite warrior who joined David's military at Ziklag. He soon became a member of David's 30 mighty men, and afterward became their captain. The great city Gibeon was inhabited by Amorites and Hivites, of Hamitic descent (Gen. 10:15-17; 2 Sam. 21:2; 1 Chron. 12:1-4).

Araunah was a Jebusite land proprietor who sold King David a threshing floor upon which to erect an altar. This site later became the foundation for Solomon's temple (Gen. 10:6,15-16; 2 Sam. 24:18-24; 1 Chron. 21:15-28).

The Queen of Sheba was the powerful leader over a wealthy nation rich in gold and precious stones, a prominent player in international trade and commerce (1 Kings 10; 2 Chron. 9). She is purported by historians to be Queen Makeda, known among the Ethiopians as "dawn upon the land."[5] Josephus, Origen, and Jerome attest that this great, intelligent woman was black, for Seba was the son and Sheba was the grandson of Cush. They maintain that out of her union with Solomon came Menelech I (Menelik), who reigned over Ethiopia.

Queen Jezebel was from Tyre of the Zidonians. She married King Ahab of Israel, contaminating the land with her Baal-worship for more than 40 years. Jezebel was destroyed by the Word of the Lord through the mouth of the prophet Elijah (Gen. 10:6,15; 1 Kings 16:31; 18:21).

The prophet Isaiah described the Ethiopians as men of stature, powerful and regal (Is. 45:14).

The Rechabites (Jer. 35) were used as models of righteousness in Jeremiah's day.[6] They can be traced to the Hivites, sons of Canaan, grandsons of Ham.

Jehudi, whose grandfather was named Cushi, was a secretary in the palace court in the time of Jeremiah. He received the sacred scroll at the hand of Baruch and later read it in the hearing of King Jehoiakim (Jer. 36:14-23).

Ebed-melech, an Ethiopian eunuch, interceded for and then delivered the prophet Jeremiah who had been thrown into a dungeon. God singled out Ebed-Melech for special commendation and a pledge of protection (Jer. 38:7-13; 39:15-18).

The minor prophet Zephaniah was a man of color, for he was the son of Cushi, which means "black" (Zeph. 1:1). Note also that the great Judean king Hezekiah was the great-grandfather of Cushi.

It is obvious that the Old Testament is filled with the rich history of people of color. What about the New Testament?

Mary, the mother of Jesus, was a distant relative of David and Solomon through her father Heli. These men were of the lineage of Boaz, a direct son of the Canaanite woman Rahab (see Ruth 4:13,20-22; Mt. 1:5-6; Lk. 3:23, 31-32).

The diplomatic wise men of the East were men of color, descendants of Midian through Abraham's dark-skinned wife Keturah (Gen. 25:1-6; Judg. 6:3; Mt. 2:1-11). Gold, frankincense, and myrrh were plentiful in Southern Arabia and East Africa. There were not simply three of these wise men, nor did they go to Bethlehem. These learned men went to Nazareth two years later to see the young child. Perhaps this caravan brought such an abundance of gifts that Jesus never had to ask for an offering during His entire earthly ministry! Tradition says that one of the wise men was Balthazar, a black man from Sheba.

It is believed that Simon the Canaanite, one of the 12 apostles of the Lamb, was black (Gen. 10:6; Mt. 10:4).

The roots of the Syrophoenician woman, whose persistent faith led to the deliverance of her daughter, can be traced to Ham (Mk. 7:24-30).

Jesus used the examples of the widow of Sidon and Naaman the Syrian (both were people of color) in the days of Elisha to rebuke Israel of His day for its religious hypocrisy. Compare also His illustrations of the men of Nineveh and the queen of the south (Sheba) who came to hear the wisdom of Solomon (Mt. 12:41-42; Lk. 4:25-27).

Simon of Cyrene carried the cross of Jesus. Cyrene was a city of Libya on the coast of North Africa, where present-day Tripoli stands. Although this passage has been misused to indicate a subservient role, no man was honored more than this man (Mt. 10:41; Lk. 23:26).

Simon was the father of Rufus, Paul's co-worker, whose mother Paul adopted as his own (Mk. 15:21; Rom. 16:13).

Hamitic countries were represented on the Day of Pentecost (Acts 2:10-11).

God interrupted the citywide revival in Samaria so that Philip the evangelist could minister to one black man, the Ethiopian eunuch (Acts 8:26-31). This powerful, wealthy man was Ethiopia's secretary of the treasury, and he later shared the gospel with Queen Candace. Church historians purport that he became the founder of the Ethiopian church. Someone has noted, "The Ethiopian eunuch was reading from a Jewish Bible in a Roman province when the Spirit of the Lord directed a Greek man to preach Jesus unto him."[7]

Simeon, called "Niger," was one of the prophetic presbyters who laid hands on Barnabas and Saul at the church of Antioch, the place where believers were first called "Christians" (Acts 11:26; 13:1-3). The English word *Negro* was borrowed from the Spanish and Portugese word for "black." Lucius of Cyrene (North Africa), his fellow minister, was also a man of color. Thus, two of the three prophetic presbyters who ordained and commissioned Barnabas and Saul (Paul) to go from the church at Antioch and take the gospel to Europe were men of color!

The Cyrenes, descendants of Ham through Phut, preached the lordship of Jesus to the Grecians, the sons of Japheth (Acts 11:20).

Apollos, a native of the land of Ham, was an eloquent preacher and leader in the church at Corinth (Acts 18:24).

Alexander, who was with Paul at Ephesus, could have been the son of Simon of Cyrene (Mk. 15:21; Acts 19:33).

The great literary apostle Paul, who penned (if one includes Hebrews) 14 of the 27 New Testament canonical books, was mistaken for an Egyptian, a black-skinned descendant of Ham. Paul, like Mordecai in the Book of Esther, was a Benjamite (Esth. 2:5; Acts 21:37-39; Phil. 3:5), a descendant of Kish (Cush?). Some identify "Kish" coming on the scene in world history as an ancient city of Mesopotamia occupied by Cushites.

We have briefly investigated the importance of people of color in the Old and New Testaments. Now what does the historical record confirm regarding their contributions?

History's Witness

Again, our purpose is not to elevate any one race above another; it is, rather, to create a fresh and broader awareness of truth among all peoples. Moreover, we are limiting our thoughts primarily to one group of people of color to enlighten the reader with regard to history as well as the Scriptures. A separate book of history could be written to acknowledge and address injustices toward native Americans and other minorities as well as their many contributions to society and history.

Ps. 68:31, KJV

> *Princes shall come out of Egypt; Ethiopia shall soon stretch out her hands unto God.*

The words of the Psalmist have been fulfilled throughout our world and national history. It is an indisputable fact that Christianity experienced an early and fruitful establishment in North Africa, Egypt, and Ethiopia. The North African and Ethiopian churches were the leading churches in the second century.

At least 9 of the 18 or 20 most prominent leaders in post New Testament Christianity were African, including Clement, Origen, Tertullian, Cyprian, Dionysius, Athanasius, Didymus, Augustine, and Cyril. Augustine, recognized as the father of theology, was also the Bishop of Hippo, a North African region. Origen, born in Alexandria, Egypt, was a prolific writer and a powerful preacher. Tertullian, born in Carthage, Africa, was one of the greatest of the early Church apologists. Anthropology supports that the people of Carthage and Egypt were unquestionably dark-complexioned before the conquest of the Arabs in the seventh century.[8]

From the perspective of American history, more than 350 blacks served our nation in the governments of at least eight southern states between the years 1869–1901; not as sanitation workers or menial laborers, but in positions such as speaker of the house, acting president of the senate, lieutenant-governor, state treasurer, senator, congressman, superintendent of public education, and commissioner of public works. At one time, there was an all-black delegation in the Congress for South Carolina. It is sad that these things are rarely taught in American history classes.[9]

It would be impossible to place within the covers of one book an account of all persons of black descent who have made a significant contribution to history. However, I wish to highlight one person from each of several special fields of endeavor: Marian Anderson, concert singer; Mary McLeod Bethune, educator; Harry T. Burleigh, composer; George Washington Carver, scientist; Charles Drew, physician; Paul Dunbar, poet; John H. Johnson, businessman; Thurgood Marshall, justice; and Martin Luther King, Jr., clergyman.[10]

Marian Anderson was known as the world's greatest contralto. Born in Philadelphia at the turn of this century, she later joined the Baptist Church and began to sing in the choir at the age of 13. As an adult, she became famous singing in Europe, and later was in demand all over the world for concerts. Her concert in front of the Lincoln memorial on Easter morning in 1939 before 75,000 people stands as a landmark in the struggle for equal rights.

This international musical ambassador from the U.S. was named in 1958 by President Eisenhower to the United States delegation to the United Nations.

Mary McLeod Bethune grew up on a farm near Mayesville, South Carolina. She was educated at the Mayesville Institute and Scotia Seminary in Concord, North Carolina. She later met D.L. Moody and studied at the Moody Bible Institute in Chicago. She followed this by teaching at Haines Normal Institute in Augusta, Georgia, and Kindell Institute in Sumter. Wanting a school of her own, she began one in Daytona Beach, Florida, on October 3, 1904. Daytona Institute grew and prospered. In 1922 it was combined with Cookman College for Boys in Jacksonville to become Bethune-Cookman College.

Harry T. Burleigh loved music from his childhood, when his voice was first discovered and cultivated. He was granted a scholarship to the National Conservatory of Music in New York City. This talented young musician became soloist at St. George's Episcopal Church and Temple Emanu-El, the richest Jewish synagogue in the nation. He later toured England and sang for King Edward VII. Burleigh also wrote music for 200 songs, several festival anthems, and a book of Negro spirituals.

George Washington Carver was born in 1864 near Diamond Grove, Missouri, to slave parents on a large plantation. He worked his way through high school in Kansas, attended Simpson College in Iowa, and received a bachelor's and master's degree from the Iowa State College of Agriculture. This brilliant young man then joined Booker T. Washington and began to teach at Tuskegee Institute in Alabama. His genius and ardent prayer life produced some 300 products from the lowly peanut!

Dr. Charles R. Drew was responsible for discovering blood plasma, a derivative of whole blood. This unprecedented procedure was responsible for saving many soldiers on battlefields and many others who have experienced accidents. Ironically, Dr. Drew's medical career came to an end following an automobile accident. He could not get hospital treatment or blood plasma in that North Carolina area—that particular local hospital and its services were for whites only in those days.

Paul Lawrence Dunbar, born in 1872, began to write verses in rhyme at the age of seven. As a young adult, his writing flourished, and his poetry was published. His first book, *Oak and Ivy*, contained 56 poems. He later published *Majors and Minors* and *Lyrics of Lowly Life*, his best known work.

John H. Johnson's childhood included a small Arkansas farm and life in Chicago during the Depression. He became the president of Johnson Publishing Company and the publisher-editor of *Ebony*, a magazine begun in 1945 for the black community. In 1951 he began *Jet*, the nation's only weekly black magazine.

In 1940 Thurgood Marshall, a young black lawyer, began his mission toward justice for all. He was educated at Lincoln University in Pennsylvania and Howard University Law School. Marshall became legal counsel for the NAACP and solicitor general for the United Nations. Marshall was chosen in 1967 as Associate Justice of the

U.S. Supreme Court. One of his landmark cases was *Brown v. Topeka Board of Education*, which brought an end to the so-called "separate but equal" educational facilities for black children in public schools throughout the nation.

Dr. Martin Luther King, Jr., was the son of a sharecropper and Baptist minister. Young Martin became a man of vision and righteous protest. Born in Atlanta, Georgia, in 1929, King graduated from Morehouse College and received advanced degrees from Crozer Theological Seminary and Boston University. Ordained in 1947, Dr. King became pastor of the prestigious Dexter Avenue Baptist Church in Montgomery, Alabama. He became a civil rights activist in 1955 following that famous day when Rosa Parks refused to give up her seat on the public bus. The Southern Christian Leadership Conference (SCLC) was established in 1957 with King as its first president. This organization sought an end to racial discrimination through nonviolent means.

The era of 1955–1965 climaxed in 1963 with the famous "March on Washington" and King's "I Have a Dream" speech at the Lincoln Memorial. In 1964 Dr. King became the youngest recipient of the Nobel Peace Prize. At approximately 6 p.m., April 4, 1968, Dr. Martin Luther King, Jr., was slain by an assassin's bullet while standing on the balcony of his room at the Lorraine Motel in Memphis, Tennessee. Although Dr. King was taken from us, his words live on: "I have a dream my four little children will one day live in a nation where they will not be judged by the color of their skin but by the content of their character."[11]

For centuries, blacks have made important contributions to American culture. Their achievements in various fields, including politics, science, athletics, music, and the arts, have played a significant role in the shaping of our modern society. From Crispus Attucks, whose death marked the start of the Revolutionary War, to the life-saving surgical procedure developed by Dr. Daniel Hale Williams, black historical figures have played an integral, yet often unheralded, part in American history.[12]

If all the deeds of courageous, noble, creative black men and women were to be mentioned, volumes upon volumes would be filled. Blacks were with George Washington as he crossed the Delaware. Benjamin Banneker helped to design the layout for the nation's capital, Washington, D.C. Harriet Tubman, called the "Moses" of her people, escaped slavery and eventually freed some 300 slaves. She claimed to be led and guided by God through visions and dreams.

Dr. Daniel Hale Williams, the pioneer black surgeon, performed the world's first open heart surgery in 1893. Lewish Latimer, a black inventor, worked with Thomas Edison and Alexander Graham Bell in drawing up the plans for the first telephone. In 1909, Matthew A. Henson was the first man to reach the North Pole. Henry Tanner was an outstanding religious painter. Great orators like Frederick Douglas and W.E.B. DuBois made lasting impressions upon their audiences.

Jack Johnson became the undisputed heavyweight boxing champion of the world in 1908. Joe Louis, the "Brown Bomber," retired as champion in 1949. Althea Gibson won the Wimbledon tennis singles title in 1957-58.

Jesse Owens was one of the greatest athletes of the twentieth century. Jackie Robinson broke through the baseball color barrier in 1947. Across the sports spectrum, some of the greatest athletes in the world are men and women of color, as was attested by the recent 1996 Olympic Games.[13]

We can but mention a few of the outstanding black Christian leaders, past and present. Richard Allen formed the African Methodist Episcopal (A.M.E.) Church in 1816. The Pentecostal outpouring was led at the turn of this century by great men such as William Seymour (1870–1922), pastor of the Azusa Street Mission, and Charles H. Mason (1866–1961), founder and general overseer of the Church of God in Christ. In 1970 Bishop J.O. Patterson helped to pioneer the C.H. Mason Theological Seminary and its systems of extension schools in Atlanta, Georgia.[14]

The contemporary scene is marked by a fresh awareness among all God's children of their worth in Christ. Freshly armed and equipped with the truth of God's Word, men and women from every quarter are boldly stepping forward into dynamic roles of leadership.

God has honored the works and words of many today, including Barbara Amos, Lorraine Austin, Luther Blackwell, Charles Blake, Shirley Caesar, Jesse Dixon, Creflo Dollar, Steve Everett, Kingsley Fletcher, Michael Goings, the late Leonard Heroo, E.V. Hill, T.D. Jakes, Ben Kinchlow, Eddie Long, Myles Munroe, Peter and Patricia Morgan, Paul Morton, Willie Murray, Turnel Nelson, G.E. Patterson, Carlton Pearson, Frederick Price, Ernestine Reems, the late Ida Robinson, the late L.O. Sanders, and

Nellie Williams, not to mention the many other outstanding leaders among predominantly black denominations. The anointing of the Holy Ghost is being poured out upon all flesh, regardless of its color!

The biblical and historial records are clear with regard to people of color. But there are many practical questions that must also be answered. For example, what do the Scriptures say about interracial marriages? Most importantly, what can we begin to do now that will end racism in these endtimes?

Chapter Nine

Ending Racism in the Endtimes

"Till we all come in the unity of the faith...."

Ephesians 4:13

The past two chapters have dealt with the second of the three prejudices—the issue of race. Having clearly examined the biblical and historical records, we have rediscovered that Ham was blessed, not cursed. Through the centuries people of color have been mightily anointed of God.

But what about the endtimes? Will the wall of racism ever be completely torn down? What about the day-to-day, pragmatic applications of these truths? There is one practical area that must be particularly addressed. What does the Bible have to say specifically about interracial marriages?

The answer is...nothing.

That's the point. Interracial marriage is not a controversy with God as it is with men. Where the Word of God says much, we are to say much. Where the Bible says little, we are to say little. By and large, those who "push" for or against interracial marriages have a problem with racial prejudice.

One of the most notable examples of interracial marriage in the Scriptures is that of Moses and his dark-skinned wife Zipporah, daughter of Jethro, the priest of Midian. Another example is the red-haired, freckled-face David and his black wife Bathsheba to whom King Solomon was born. Obviously, the most distinguished Child born to a "mixed union" was the Lord Jesus Christ. His mother was Mary and His father was the Holy Ghost! By God's design Jesus was a perfect blend of the human and divine natures, very God and very man.

Nowhere does any Scripture prohibit interracial marriage, but there are practical consequences to prayerfully consider before any marriage, as noted by apostle Paul in First Corinthians 7:28, "Nevertheless such shall have trouble [pressure] in the flesh...."

In Deuteronomy 7:1-4 God did forbid His people to intermarry with the heathen nations of Canaan. However, this injunction was not because they were of a different race, but a different *heart*. They worshiped idols. Children of God may not marry those who worship idol gods, regardless of skin color.

Can a person of any race or nation become a child of God in Christ? Of course. Does it then displease God for His children to intermarry?

In Exodus 12:48-49, when those of other races and nations came into covenantal relationship with Israel by circumcision (a type of salvation and water baptism in the New Testament), one law then applied to them all! The first chapter of Matthew reveals this principle, noting the many different nationalities in the genealogy of Jesus.

Is. 1:18, KJV

...Though your sins be as scarlet, they shall be as white as snow; though they be red like crimson, they shall be as wool.

As discussed, all nations were created of one blood. If any "color" is seen by God, it is the color of sin, and not the color of skin. God does see color. He made color, but He does not judge or discriminate because of color. The "unequal yoke" mentioned by Paul in Second Corinthians 6:14 refers to a believer in Christ being in covenant with an unbeliever, a sinner. An unequal yoke is not found among believers who intermarry regardless of their race or color. These requirements for marriage are set forth by the truth of God's Word, not the fearful traditions of men.

Has the Lord renewed the spirit of your mind to the point that you can accept intermarriage between blacks and whites? Few parents want to think about this, for few could handle such a relationship developing in their homes. But there is nowhere in all the Word of God that He implies that men of any race have any inherent differences. *All* have sinned and come short of the glory of God (Rom. 3:23). Color has never mattered to God. He completely overlooks it. Color has nothing to do with one's sin or salvation. As a Christian father, I don't want any of my children to marry a sinner of any color.

Another writer addresses this issue:

"Have you ever examined yourself for the cancerous growth of prejudice? You don't realize how prejudiced you are until you mingle with one another. Prejudice rarely surfaces or comes out into the open, as long as you stay and live with your 'own kind.' Racial prejudice surfaces quickly when you get into close quarters with people of other races. The acid test which will quickly measure your hidden prejudices comes when your child brings another child home from another racial group (specifically, Black and White). As you sit together over dinner, what emotions do you feel as you think about the possibility of your guest from another race becoming your son-in-law or daughter-in-law? Can you picture yourself bouncing your grandchildren from this union on your knee? Whatever is in you, my friend, is going to come out. We cannot be all that God desires us to be with any degree of prejudice in us at all."[1]

People from other nations, cultures, and places marry all the time. Irish, Asian, German, French, Spanish, Puerto Rican— these marriages are usually not considered interracial. The contention seems to arise whenever blacks and whites are involved.

For centuries prejudiced men have used First Kings 11:1-2 to condemn interracial marriage. Whites need to remember that Solomon, to whom these words were spoken, was the son of his black mother Bathsheba. The main point is that God was warning Solomon against mingling with and marrying foreign women who would turn his heart away from God unto idols. It doesn't matter what color friends or lovers are— if they are going to turn your heart away from loving and serving the Lord, say good-bye.

1 Cor. 7:28, NIV

...But those who marry will face many troubles in this life, and I want to spare you this.

1 Cor. 7:28, AMP

...Yet those who marry will have physical and earthly troubles....

1 Cor. 7:28, TLB

...Marriage will bring extra problems that I wish you didn't have to face right now.

There are practical questions that must be addressed with regard to interracial marriages.

First, is this the will of God for your life? Some marry into other races just to make a point. These persons are not prejudiced, yet they seem to have to prove to themselves and to others that they are not biased and can indeed marry outside of their race. Some of these have set forth their marriage as a badge of honor. Be careful that your marriage does not become an ornament of self-righteousness.

Second, have you considered the consequences with regard to you, and your mate, and especially the children born of your union? Some of your friends or members of your family may not know the Lord or the Scriptures. Others may be prejudiced and not understand the mercy of God. Jesus reminded us in Luke 14:28 to really "count the cost" in whatever we do.

I am not trying to promote interracial marriage; neither am I against it. I want to give you the good Word of God so that you can make wise decisions. Arguing against interracial marriage is usually the indication of racial prejudice. God created all the races, and He loves people of all colors. Because of rampant ignorance and bigotry in our society, those believers who intermarry (and the children they bear) will have pressures in the flesh. But if they are in Christ, He will bless their union in spite of men.

Racism and the Endtimes

The Charismatic movement, or renewal, was basically a move of the Spirit among white middle-class Americans in suburban and small-town areas. Very few black Americans were affected by this move of the Spirit; nor were other ethnic groups unless they fell into the middle-class status.[2]

Since the 1960s and 70s, there has been an unprecedented outpouring of the Holy Ghost upon all races. This rain from Heaven has prepared the global harvest for the end-time Feast of Tabernacles. The gospel of the Kingdom shall be preached to all "nations" (Mt. 24:14)— this is the Greek word *ethnos*— to all ethnic groups, to all races! King Jesus will not return to this planet until this matter of racism is dealt with! Christians of diverse denominations and racial backgrounds will come into unity and fellowship. This unity is not only a desire but a demand of our Lord. As His Church, we cannot continue to contribute to the problem of disunity by inadvertently causing dissension and division.

Eph. 4:13, KJV

Till we all come in the unity of the faith....

The Lord's coming is not "any minute"; the key word is "till" (compare Ps. 110:1; Acts 3:19-21; Jas. 5:7). He is coming for a unified and glorified Church. We must abolish racist attitudes, concepts, policies, and practices among the remnant of true Christians and local churches. We must achieve unity in the eyes of the Lord.

Jesus will remain where He is— at the right hand of the Father— until the enemy of racism is under His feet (Acts 2:32-35; Rom. 16:20). That awful foe was birthed and raised to maturity in the Church through the evil that lurks among us and in us. Racism must be exposed, subdued, and brought under subjection to our King. The end-time Church is His Body, and our feet will tread down every enemy!

So what must we do to accomplish this? One of my close friends and ministerial colleagues has given us the answer. His writings on the subject are the clearest and most anointed that I have found.

He offers 12 practical principles for exposing and eliminating the great prejudice of racism:[3]

1. See and treat racism as the sin that it is (Acts 10:34; Jas. 2:1).

2. Renounce and repent of prejudice and racist attitudes so you can help free others (Mt. 7:2,5; 2 Cor. 10:3-5).

3. Confront every form of racism in your relationships (Ezek. 2:6-7; Gal. 2:11-12).

4. See people as God does and refuse to know anyone after the flesh (1 Sam. 16:7; 2 Cor. 5:16-17).

5. Accept divinely predetermined individual ethnic uniqueness (Ps. 139:14; Jer. 1:5; 13:23).

6. Christian employers or managers should hire, promote, or dismiss people based on character and competency, not race or gender (2 Sam. 23:3; 1 Tim. 5:21).

7. Fellowship with Christians of different races and cultures (Prov. 18:24; Acts 2:42; 1 Jn. 1:7).

8. Sponsor and support seminars and symposiums on racism (Prov. 11:14; Is. 1:18; Acts 15:5-6).

9. Submit to the Holy Spirit if He impresses you to join a church pastored by someone of a different race (Jer. 3:15; 1 Cor. 12:18; Gal. 3:28).

10. Do not support churches or organizations that practice racism (Ezek. 12:1-3; 1 Cor. 5:11; 2 Cor. 6:17-18).

11. Intercede for all leaders in regard to racial harmony in the Church (2 Chron. 7:14; Eph. 6:18-20; 1 Tim. 2:1-2).

12. Forgive everyone who has hurt you through their racism (Mt. 6:12-15; 18:21-22; Col. 3:12-14).

Throughout the family of God, we have sought to categorize people. Even in our worship styles, we must understand the difference between ethnicity and acquired culture. Prejudice is not an inclination towards or against certain kinds of food, or clothing, or music—these are preferences and are a fact of life because we are each different. Preference is not prejudice.

Only God through the power of His Word and Spirit can deal with the sin of racism. The world is teaching integration. The Bible teaches reconciliation. The beginnings of real reconciliation will require the dismantling and disintegration of all those things that stand against it. A mature Church and people will be marked by their ability to distinguish and discern God's work apart from all others. It's not enough to play with this predicament with a room full of blacks and whites who are really saying in their hearts, "You can make us sit next to each other, but you can't make me love you!"

In the closing words of this same godly pastor,

"The disease of racism is invading the Church family, and it is too serious to ignore or sweep under the rug of religious indifference. God is demanding that the Church acknowledge her sin and rise up to rid herself of this deadly evil. There are no neutral bystanders in this struggle. You and I can either be part of the problem or part of the solution! Since God has declared His position, He is forcing us to choose. Will we stand with God and oppose racism wherever we find it, or will we stand apart from Him and apart from His blessings? It is time to get busy. There is a worldwide family of grace to embrace and unite in Christ!"[4]

How do we overcome racial prejudice? Put a "g" in front of "race" and you get "grace." Grace is bigger than race! The King-Priest of Jesus ministers to all men, to all races. Jesus is color-blind. There is no racial prejudice in His more excellent ministry. All races and nations shall serve Him (Ps. 72:10-11; Is. 11:11-12).

The first two of the three prejudices under consideration have dealt with gender and race. These are obvious areas of human need. There remains one final subtle hurdle that few are willing to address— national prejudice— the issue of Jew and Greek.

Part Four

From National Prejudice to One Holy Nation

"…an holy nation…."

1 Peter 2:9

Foreword by
Dr. Michael L. Brown

One of the greatest enemies of prejudice is truth. Prejudice is fueled by lies, misunderstanding, and suspicion. Truth destroys the divisive myths of prejudice, and everyone who wants to combat those myths must be a lover of truth, that includes being a seeker of truth. Kelley Varner is both a lover of truth and a seeker of truth.

When I was first asked to write the foreword to this section, I responded, "I'm the wrong man for this. Based on what I've read, Kelley and I see the issues of Israel and the Church very differently." I thought that would end things. After all, Kelley Varner is an established author and long-time student of the Word; why would he pursue the matter any further? Yet that is not the attitude of one who *really* loves the truth and therefore seeks it. After hearing my response, this man gave himself to serious reflection and study, and he recognized some blind spots in his position—just as I have often uncovered blind spots in some of my own positions over the years. (By the way, if you have never reconsidered or modified any of your views on any doctrinal or interpretive issues, I question whether you are truly growing in your knowledge of the

Lord and His Word.) What better way to demonstrate one's opposition to prejudice and misunderstanding?

Now, anyone who has carefully studied the Scriptures on the subject of the Church and the Jewish people knows that there are several standard lines of interpretation that are normally followed and numerous thorny problems that must be tackled. Has the Church replaced Israel? Must either Israel or the Church be removed before God can deal with them? Kelley Varner says no to both of these questions, enabling him to argue strongly for God's *one* ultimate purpose summed up in *one* people in Jesus. With this overall position I completely agree.

Of course, there are certain points that I would emphasize differently than Pastor Varner. I would emphasize that Jesus Christ was a Jew in His humanity, whereas in His eternal nature He is neither Jew nor Gentile. I interpret the Olive Tree of Romans 11 to represent the Patriarchs and Israel, rather than Jesus. Also, I view Jewish believers in Jesus to be "true Jews" or "spiritual Israel" (as opposed to all believers in Jesus the Messiah being described as such). Therefore, though we both see the Church as consisting of Israel and the nations, I would not see the Church as the greater Israel. And because *Palestine* is a later, non-biblical term coined by the Romans, I do not view Deuteronomy 29–30 as the "Palestinian Covenant." In my opinion, these chapters are primarily the heritage of Israel itself, including the promise of the Land.

However, differences such as these are the very substance out of which useful dialogue and interaction arise, and I wholeheartedly join with and affirm my brother in his efforts to remove all destructive walls of partition while allowing for distinctiveness in calling and identity. May truth triumph, and may God make His people one.

Chapter Ten

A People Belonging to God

"...a holy nation, a people belonging to God...."

1 Peter 2:9, NIV

Christ is not prejudiced. His Spirit transcends every man-made boundary. He is not a sexist or a racist. Neither is He a respecter of nations. The third of the three great prejudices is national prejudice—Christ is neither Jew nor Greek.

Thankfully, over the past few years men have been speaking to the issue of racial prejudice in the Body of Christ with some measure of sensitivity and repentance. Moreover, the walls that divide men and women (especially with regard to public ministry) are finally beginning to be exposed and addressed. But the mountain of misunderstanding between Jews and non-Jews is fallow ground that has yet to be plowed, intelligently addressed, and ultimately resolved.

Prejudice is not preference, as exampled by our varied choices of food, clothing, or musical styles. We all differ from one another with regard to our personal tastes. In Christ there is neither male nor female, yet we are grateful for the distinctions. In Him there is neither black nor white, yet men remain black or white. I, a white male, cannot fully comprehend the hateful attitudes and perpetrated injustices toward those who are not my gender or color. Yet as a minister of the gospel, I can labor to bring an end to these inequities by boldly declaring the Word of God.

Finally, in Christ there is neither Jew nor Greek; but there is *still* Jew, and there is *still* Greek (gentile), and we are different! I am not a Jew by nationality or race, and thus I cannot fully feel the heart of my brother who is. Most of us "Greeks" are woefully ignorant of the rich legacy of Jewish history. Let us value Jewish culture, custom, and ethnicity. Let us appreciate and learn more about our mutual spiritual heritage in the Old Testament Scriptures. As we do, let us maintain that the most powerful commonality between Jew and Greek is based upon the saving blood of the Messiah Jesus Christ. God has not called either group to renounce their nationalities or basic cultural preferences, but to focus upon the cross of Christ, the cause of the Kingdom, and the love for each other that Jesus promised would be the identifying feature of His true disciples (Jn. 13:35).

Jesus adds and multiplies, while the devil subtracts and divides. Paul clearly exemplifies this principle in his Epistles. In the fourteenth chapter of Paul's letter to the Romans, the apostle wisely shows our Christian liberty with regard to the eating of restricted meat and the observance of certain holy days. Each of us is to be persuaded in our own minds while granting our brother the same privilege. The issue is not "either/or," but rather "both/and." The former attitude builds walls; the latter tears them down. As gentiles, we must recognize our brothers, the Jews. So must our brothers recognize the position God has afforded us in His family and in His plan.

For too long we have allowed a spirit of religiosity to keep us from recognizing the heart of God for His people. In many cases, we have allowed our personal theologies and eschatological beliefs to cover and propagate our private prejudice. The Jews did not "miss their chance" with Christ's crucifixion. As we shall examine later in this chapter, it was always God's intention to extend His gift of salvation to the gentiles. And God has not rejected the Jews from His plan and purpose, as Paul speaks to so clearly in his Epistle to the Romans.

The accusations or acts of ignorant men who want to label the Jews as "Christ killers" cannot nullify God's love or purpose for Israel or the Jews. Nor must we as gentile believers hang our heads as "second-class citizens" in the plan and purpose of God. As God's Spirit is moving and calling us to tear down the walls that divide, we must recognize that this third wall, the "middle wall of partition," must also come tumbling down so that each may be released and restored to his place in the "household of God" (see Eph. 2:11-19).

While researching and re-reading this present manuscript, I was influenced through the writings of Dr. Michael Brown and others. The Spirit of the Lord made me painfully aware of my own personal omissions in this area. I had to honestly ask these questions, "Am I unconsciously guilty of national prejudice? Am I for the Jews with the same intensity as I am for women and people of color?"

Although I have had no personal desire or ambition to champion the rights of anyone, while writing this book I felt the Spirit's heartfelt cry for the restoration of full spiritual rights in Christ for all women and minorities. I received an apostolic burden to dismantle gender prejudice and racial prejudice throughout the nations.

Then I arrived at the foot of this third dividing wall, and initially, I found myself turning to my own eschatological concerns. Yet, God is out to destroy all dividing walls. The fruits of God's current moves of revival are proof of His design. In fact, individual doctrinal issues will always be with us until we allow the fires of revival to lift us beyond our petty differences into our unity in Jesus Christ. God wants to remove every exclusionary boundary we have built to separate us from others in the Body of Christ. As we tear down this wall of national prejudice, we must also not overlook the other "national" prejudices that have kept us separated and at enmity with one another. God also wants to break down the dividing walls of our own "imagi-nations" and "denomi-nations," those man-made divisions based upon the opinions and interpretations of individuals and institutions.

God wants the Body of Christ to be a place where His presence can dwell and flow freely, unhindered by prejudice of any kind. He is not a respecter of persons or cultures. He is the creative Author of culture, and He is looking for a people from every culture to be willing vessels who will allow Him to express His life and glory as He has created them to. Unfortunately, the Church has struggled with this concept since its earliest days. God made it clear to the first apostles: God does not require the Jew to become a gentile in order to serve Him; neither should the non-Jew in Christ feel inferior to his Jewish brethren. He should not feel compelled to become a Jew and take on Jewish ethnic customs and culture to be able to take his place in the purposes or God or to become an heir to God's promise and blessing. Yet God does call us to love and respect one another and not to hinder His work in our brothers in Christ. Jew and Greek must embrace one another in unity and allow God's Spirit and purpose to be expressed and flourish in their respective cultures and walk together in obedience to God's commands.

Jew or Greek, "circumcision" or "uncircumcision," is not an issue in Christ. Dr. Michael Brown, a dynamic voice to the Body of Christ, clearly addresses this point:

"In First Corinthians Paul stated in no uncertain terms that 'Circumcision is nothing and uncircumcision is nothing. Keeping God's commands is what counts' (1 Cor. 7:19, NIV)...

"As far as salvation and relating to God is concerned, circumcision carries no weight at all. But Paul also had this to say: 'Was a man already circumcised when he was called? He should not become uncircumcised. Was a man uncircumcised when he was called? He should not be circumcised...Each one should remain in the situation which he was in when God called him' (1 Cor. 7:18, 20, NIV).

"This is pretty clear too. A Jew who becomes saved should continue to live as a Jew, just as a man who becomes saved continues to live as a man and a woman who becomes saved continues to live as a woman. The Jew who becomes born from above must cast off all death-giving traditions. He must throw aside all feelings of superiority. He must put no trust in his heritage. He must enter into new life in the Spirit. He must boast in Jesus and the cross alone. But he should continue to live as a Jew—wherever it does not contradict the Word or hinder the Spirit's flow." [1]

I pray that you will hear my heart. While finishing Chapters Ten and Eleven, I became gripped with a fresh burden for the Jewish people. Like the apostle Paul, my desire is that they will receive Jesus as their true Messiah. At this point, I do not fully know how the Lord will work out this enlarged commission through my life and ministry, but I now know that He has also charged me to bridge the gap between Jew and Greek.

I have been an Old Testament preacher for almost 30 years. I've written 17 volumes of commentaries covering the Old Testament Books of Genesis through Ezekiel, as well as Habakkuk and Haggai. One of my first books was on the tabernacle of Moses, which is the grandfather clause of all biblical understanding. The Levitical economy, including our understanding about the feasts of the Lord and the various offerings, is foundational to our Christian faith. Every Christian needs to experience and appreciate his roots—the Old Testament history and faith of the people of Abraham! Through the work of Jesus upon the cross, we have become heirs to their legacy.

We are not replacing Old Testament Israel with the Church, but rather we are proclaiming the rightful place of both Jew and Greek in one Body by the cross. I have long taught that God is a covenantal God who keeps His covenants. Scripture clearly shows that extending His grace and salvation to the gentile was part of His purpose from the beginning, but our becoming His sons through the work of Jesus and our inclusion into the family of God in no way nullifies His covenant to Abraham. In Christ, the Abrahamic Covenant is made bigger! Addressing the relationship between the two groups, Dr. Michael Brown also adds,

> "It would not have been a problem if gentile Christians had simply said, 'God has *expanded* the borders of Israel! Now we are included among the covenant people since we are the spiritual seed of Abraham. And we look forward to the day when the Lord will restore the physical seed of Abraham too. The Old Testament Church consisted of Israel alone, but the New Testament Church consists of Israel and us. Together we are the new Israel!' Many devout Christians have held to this belief—and there is much truth to it—without for a moment thinking that God's promises to the natural children were ever in doubt."[2]

The bottom line here is not the remaining national or cultural distinctions between the Jew and Greek. The real, underlying, and overwhelming issue has to do with the One who has joined us in one Body by the cross: Christ!

One Holy Nation From Among the Nations

1 Pet. 2:9, KJV

> *But ye are a chosen generation, a royal priesthood, an holy nation, a peculiar people; that ye should shew forth the praises of Him who hath called you out of darkness into His marvellous light.*

The Father's eternal purpose in Christ Jesus, revealed in First Peter 2:9, is to gather unto Himself a royal Family, a Race from among the races, one holy nation from among the nations, a people belonging to God.

Gal. 3:28, KJV

> *There is neither Jew nor Greek, there is neither bond nor free, there is neither male nor female: for ye are all one in Christ Jesus.*

Our theme is that God is no respecter of persons now that Christ has come. We have already established that there is neither male nor female; neither is there bond nor free in Christ. And though there is much work to be done, we are making progress in tearing down the dividing walls between the sexes and the races. We must continue to encourage women and people of color to appropriate their full callings as members of the Body of Christ. As we enter this new millennium, we must also deal with the third of the three prejudices, *national* prejudice, the belief that one nation, people, or group is greater than all others in the eyes of God—whether that nation is a geographical or a man-made one, as in "denomi-nation."

Many evangelical and Pentecostal American Christians have become unduly preoccupied and focused upon the nation of Israel—its people, land, and temple. They have created presumptuous theologies and movements that require the Church to be completely removed from the international scene before God can fulfill His covenants to the Jews. Others reject the nation and people of Israel altogether and claim that all of God's promises to Israel were completely transferred to a gentile Church and that the Jews no longer have any rights or place before God. But the New Testament makes it clear that all covenants consummate in Christ. Jesus, as the Heir of all things, confirmed and secured the covenantal promises made to the fathers—Abraham, Isaac, and Jacob (Acts 3:13; Rom. 15:8; Heb. 1:1-2). Individuals have dwelled on national distinctions that have never been part of God's intention for His people, as He clearly showed the early Church.

Acts 15:8-9, KJV

And God, which knoweth the hearts, bare them [the gentiles] *witness, giving them the Holy Ghost, even as He did unto us* [the Jews];

And put no difference between us and them, purifying their hearts by faith.

Peter, the apostle to the circumcision (the Jews), made it clear: Before God there is no difference between "us" and "them," the Jew and the Greek.

Who Is Abraham's Seed?

Mt. 1:1, KJV

> *...Jesus Christ...the son of Abraham....*

Gal. 3:16, KJV

> *Now to Abraham and his seed were the promises made. He saith not, And to seeds, as of many; but as of one, And to thy seed, which is Christ.*

The New Testament reveals that the seed of Abraham is "Christ." The apostle did not mention "seeds," a natural seed and a spiritual seed. The only seed that counted with the Lord and Paul was a *spiritual* Seed— Christ! Jesus Christ was the greatest Son of Abraham. In the same way in which mankind is both male and female, the spiritual nation of God is made up of Jew and Greek.

Abraham the Chaldean was not a Jew. Elijah the Tishbite was not a Jew. In any era, the thing that counts most with God is *faith*! Hebrews 11–12 records the history of one covenantal people throughout the ages who have come to God by faith, regardless of nationality. We are presently living in the expanded extremities of that singular, covenantal purpose. The key issue here is identity, the nature of the seed. The seed is not defined by nationality, race, gender, or culture— the seed of Abraham (Christ) has always been spiritual, determined by faith!

Again, we are not replacing Israel with the Church. The family of God in both testaments incorporates men and women of faith from every tribe, tongue, and culture. The Church, made up of both Jew and Greek, is also

Abraham's seed. The glorious, anticipated outpouring of the Spirit upon national Israel will take place in the context of the global outpouring of the Spirit upon all flesh—Israeli flesh, African flesh, Russian flesh, Chinese flesh, and even American flesh! The ongoing Messianic family, the Body of Christ, is comprised of covenantal men and women from every nation and era.

Galatians 3:19 affirms that the law (not the Church) was parenthetical, added because of the transgression. The Church is not an afterthought in the back of God's mind, but we are part of His eternal purpose and program. We are not spiritual stepchildren, but a chosen people. From the beginning God has sought out a people from among every nation, a people whose "national" characteristics are clearly outlined in the New Testament Epistles and include the following:

1. Jews inwardly (Rom. 2:28-29).

2. Children of the promise who are counted for the seed (Rom. 9:6-8).

3. The chosen (people) generation (1 Pet. 2:1-10).

4. The holy nation (Mt. 3:7-10; 21:42-43; 1 Pet. 2:9-10).

5. The circumcision (Phil. 3:3).

6. The new (heavenly) Jerusalem (Jn. 4:19-24; Gal. 4:21-31; Heb. 12:22-24; Rev. 21:1-11).

Everything said about Jesus Christ with regard to His being the Seed of Abraham can be applied to the Church, comprised of both Jew and Greek. He is the true Vine and we are the branches, the seed who prolong His days.

We are His offspring, His generation, conformed to His image and likeness. First John 4:17 succinctly sums up these truths: "...as He is, so are we in this world."

Rom. 9:6, AMP

...For it is not everybody who is a descendant of Jacob (Israel) who belongs to [the true] Israel.

The word "Hebrew" (a descendant of Eber) and "Jew" (a descendant of Judah) are essentially man-given terms. The first mention of the term "Israel" is found in Genesis 32:24-32. What happened that night to Jacob takes place in the life of every man (from any nation) who encounters the living God. In my opinion, the word *Israel* is a God-given word, and it can relate to any person in any age who has met God face to face. Such a person overcomes sin and self by experiencing a change of name (or nature). In this transformation, he becomes in his spirit an Israelite, a new creature, a prevailing prince.

Gen. 32:27-28, AMP

[The Man] asked him, What is your name? And [in shock of realization, whispering] he said, Jacob [supplanter, schemer, trickster, swindler]!

And He said, Your name shall be called no more Jacob [supplanter], but Israel [contender with God]; for you have contended and have power with God and with men, and have prevailed.

The old man, the Jacob nature, must be smitten by the Lord. God wants each of us to be overcomers, to prevail, to endure. The divine nature is displayed whenever God strikes our thigh—the place of human strength, man's ability to reproduce or create. He must increase; we must shrink or decrease. Have you met God? Has He touched you? Those who are Israelites in spirit are betrayed by their walk. There is a familiar limp in the life or ministry that is "touched" by the Lord.

In Time Past Gentiles

The second chapter of Ephesians is a panorama of redemption's plan, beginning with man as a sinner and ending with him as the habitation of God through the Spirit. Verses 11-12 particularly describe unregenerate, untamed, unsaved man.

Eph. 2:11-12, KJV

Wherefore remember, that ye being in time past Gentiles in the flesh, who are called Uncircumcision by that which is called the Circumcision in the flesh made by hands;

That at that time ye were without Christ, being aliens from the commonwealth of Israel, and strangers from the covenants of promise, having no hope, and without God in the world.

Much of popular theology and eschatology leaves us in the same predicament. According to those views, Christians are still called "gentiles" and the "uncircumcision," and are still left apart from the promises and purposes of God. Throughout the Body of Christ there are segments ("denomi-nations") who try to use man-made religious traditions and culture to identify themselves as specially favored by God to the exclusion of all others. Practically speaking, these views uplift singular groups and leave the rest of us without Christ. We remain alienated from the wealth and spiritual heritage we have in common with Abraham, Isaac, and Jacob. We are left strangers to the blessings and benefits of the Abrahamic and Davidic covenants.

Religious tradition has left us without God in the world. The distant, external God of the old religious order is no better than the impersonal God of deistic philosophy who created this universe and wound it up like a clock only to walk away to watch it run by natural law. This earth either belongs to the devil and his crowd or Jesus and His Church. Either the devil's greatest day or the Day of the Lord is now upon us—we can't have it both ways.

The Emmanuel principle pictures the Church as salt and light, the ongoing incarnation of the living Word— He *is* come in the flesh of His Body, not just one part or another. To deny that is to oppose the anointing, to offer some humanistic substitute for the truth. We are not strangers and pilgrims just passing through. There is a generation of overcomers who have come to stay and to unite in power and authority through the blood of Jesus.

Moreover, the Greek word for "gentiles" in Ephesians 2:11 is *ethnos* and means "a race (as of the same habit), a tribe; especially a foreign one (usually by implication, pagan)." Vine's adds that *ethnos* means "heathen; a multitude of people of the same nature or genus; a nation, people." Compare the English words *heathen* and *ethnic*.

Jesus is the Seed of Abraham. Abraham is our brother in Christ! As stated, the law was temporary until the coming of the promised seed—Jesus and His Body, made up of both Jew and Greek. The New Testament Church is God's chosen people, regardless of nationality. We are not second-class citizens, and there is no plan "B." We do not have to be evacuated from the planet or from history so that God can renew His program with the Jews. God has a better plan: He has determined to pour out His Spirit upon us all! Men from every nation, including Israel, are destined to constitute His chosen people, His covenantal family.

Religious traditions have tried to sew up the veil that the Savior rent, but the middle wall of partition has been abolished. Now that Jesus has come, there is neither Jew nor Greek. There are no national distinctions, and no special advantages (or disadvantages) in Him.

Phil. 3:3, AMP

> *For we [Christians] are the true circumcision, who worship God in spirit and by the Spirit of God and exult and glory and pride ourselves in Jesus Christ, and put no confidence or dependence [on what we are] in the flesh and on outward privileges and physical advantages and external appearances.*

Neither Jew nor gentile can put their confidence in outward appearance or physical advantage. Both must be born again! The Body of Christ is made up of men from every race and nation. Our true biblical identity rests in Christ alone, restoring three specific New Covenant blessings—*fellowship, promises,* and *authority.* First, we are in fellowship with the saints of the ages, who paid a great price to pass the heritage of faith on to us. Now we are to enter into our inheritance carrying the bones of Joseph, the hopes and dreams of previous generations. Second, believers cannot claim the promised inheritance until we know who we are in Christ. We must arise and possess the land (the earth), a campaign that has been previously relegated to another time (the future) and people (national Israel). Third, with the appropriation of the promises of God comes a fresh authority and boldness, a new anointing.

The Ingathering of the Stranger and Foreigner Into the Palestinian Covenant

Gen. 26:4-5, KJV

And I will make thy seed to multiply as the stars of heaven, and will give unto thy seed all these countries; and in thy seed shall all the nations of the earth be blessed;

Because that Abraham obeyed My voice, and kept My charge, My commandments, My statutes, and My laws.

Gal. 3:7-9, KJV

Know ye therefore that they which are of faith, the same are the children of Abraham.

And the scripture, foreseeing that God would justify the heathen through faith, preached before the gospel unto Abraham, saying, In thee shall all nations be blessed.

> *So then they which be of faith are blessed with faithful Abraham.*

It is clear that the inclusion of the gentiles into the blessings of Abraham was part of God's plan from the beginning.

The term "the Palestinian Covenant" is particular to traditional futurism. As such, Deuteronomy 29–30 are purported to be a confirmation and enlargement of the original Abrahamic covenant, amplifying the "land" features of that agreement.

Most prophecy teachers readily profess that the key fulfillment of end-time prophecy was the return of the Jews to their homeland and, consequently, becoming a nation again in May of 1948. That event was a remarkable, historical reality that affirmed that God has supernaturally preserved the Jewish people for His end-time purposes. From that chronological launching pad, men have been making personal predictions regarding those purposes for nearly 50 years.

Notwithstanding, Bible students still readily ask, "But what about the Palestinian Covenant of Deuteronomy 29–30? What does it mean, and is it still relevant to the Jews or the Church today?"

As previously noted, the New Testament Epistles (especially Romans, Galatians, and Ephesians) establish the true seed of Abraham to be Christ. The apostolic foundation of New Testament covenantal theology shows the Abrahamic Covenant fulfilled in Him.

So the key question that remains is: To whom was the Palestinian Covenant made? A close examination of Deuteronomy 29–30 divulges that those promises were made to both Jew and Greek. (Remember, prejudice makes decisions before having all the necessary information. What some have taught about the endtimes up till now is not necessarily wrong, but perhaps just incomplete.)

First of all, Deuteronomy 29:1 states that the Palestinian Covenant was made *outside* the natural land, in the country of Moab. (Ruth the Moabitess would later appreciate that as she entered into covenant with the one true God.) Moreover, this agreement, it is noted, was made "beside" ("apart from, aside from") the Mosaic Covenant cut in Horeb or Sinai. To reiterate, Paul plainly stated in Galatians 3:17-19 that it was the law, not grace, that was "added" or parenthetical, and that the law could not "disannul" or "invalidate" the authority of the Abrahamic Covenant fulfilled in Christ.

In Deuteronomy 29:2, Moses recounted Jehovah's complete defeat of Pharaoh, the god and prince of Egypt—a type of the devil, the god and prince of this world system. The very spirit of the Palestinian Covenant is predicated upon Jesus' complete victory over sin and satan!

But Deuteronomy 29:10-13 reveals the heart of the matter, that God loves *all* men and women. Such devotion knows no prejudice with regard to gender, race, or nationality. This passage shows that Jehovah *gathered* the captains, the elders, the officers, the men, the women, and their children, and especially the "stranger" among them to be part of a *"people unto Himself."* *All* could participate in the promise He had made to Abraham, Isaac, and Jacob! From the beginning, He has wanted a kingdom of priests, a nation from among the nations— a "people" belonging to God!

The Hebrew word for "stranger" in Deuteronomy 29:11 means "a guest or foreigner," and is translated as "alien, sojourner, stranger" in the King James Version. The Bible says much about the "stranger"; the reader is encouraged to discover these truths in both testaments (see Ex. 12:48; Num. 15:14-15; Deut. 10:19; 16:14; Josh. 8:35; Ruth 2:10; 1 Kings 8:41-43; Ezek. 44:9; Acts 2:10; Eph. 2:11-22; 1 Pet. 1:1-5).

The *key principle* for understanding the Palestinian Covenant (which heretofore has covertly fostered national prejudice) is found in verses 14-15. Here we plainly see that these promises were not made to the members of just one nation, the natural stock of Abraham.

Deut. 29:14-15, KJV

Neither with you only do I make this covenant and this oath;

But with him that standeth here with us this day before the Lord our God, and also with him that is not here with us this day.

Jehovah's contract included those who stood there that day with Israel—the Old Testament strangers; furthermore, it embraced those who were not there that day—the New Testament strangers! The "him" of verse 15 anticipates the one new Man of the New Covenant, comprised of both Jew and Greek.

Our fundamental faith avows that *all* have sinned and come short of the glory of God. *All* men were estranged in Adam, alienated from the life of God by sin. Now *all* can have an equal footing in Christ, without distinction of sex, race, or nationality! David, the man after God's own heart, summed up this truth: "For we are strangers before Thee, and sojourners, as were all our fathers..." (1 Chron. 29:15).

Many Christians are quite familiar with the blessings and cursings delineated in Deuteronomy 28. We must now understand that Chapters 29 and 30 extend out of that same landmark passage. Men boldly teach and preach from chapter 28 while relegating chapters 29–30 to another time and people. But those chapters are for us, too! Deuteronomy 29:29 declares that it is time for these blessings to be "revealed" or "uncovered," for they belong unto us and our children—regardless of nationality!

The first three verses of chapter 30 certainly prophesy Jehovah's end-time compassion upon the Jewish people. They also prophetically illustrate how the true Church, the Body of Christ, has been scattered and divided throughout the "nations"— the denomi-nations and imagi-nations of men. Indeed in these days we are witnessing a great "gathering" of God's remnant people from out of these "nations"—He is gathering His one holy nation back to the "land" of the Bible, the "land" of the Holy Ghost, back to the heavenly places in Christ Jesus.

Men have begun to "return" to the Lord. This word in Deuteronomy 30:2 is the Hebrew word for *restoration*, and it means "to turn back (to the starting point)." For the Church, the starting point is *Jesus*! He is the Alpha, the Beginning, the Author of our faith. God will have such a people turn to Him with all their heart, obeying

Him by the inward law of a new nature and a new creation. This is the New Testament law of the spirit of life in Christ Jesus wrought by the power and enabling of the Holy Ghost.

As God gathers His people unto Himself from throughout the denomi-nations and the imagi-nations, He has promised to do us good (see Deut. 30:5-6). Deuteronomy 30:6 strikes the keynote of this entire section, for God knew that a *spiritual* circumcision of the *heart* was the primary truth of all covenantal relationship with Himself (see Rom. 2:28-29; Gal. 5:6; 6:15; Col. 2:1-12; 3:10-11).[3]

The Palestinian Covenant closes in Deuteronomy 30:20 by emphasizing its primary aim: God wants a nation from among the nations, a people for Himself, "*He is thy life*" (compare Ps. 27:1; 36:9; Jn. 11:25; 14:6; 17:3; Acts 17:28; Gal. 2:20; Col. 3:3; Rev. 22:1). This great Deuteronomic covenant is for *all* men who will enter in, as well as the nation of Israel. It was as powerful in its workings for the "stranger" as it was for those descendants of Abraham who stood before Moses that day. Paul concluded the matter in Ephesians 2:19-22 when he said:

> *Now therefore ye are no more strangers and foreigners, but fellowcitizens with the saints, and of the household of God...In whom ye* [both Jew and Greek] *also are builded together for an habitation of God through the Spirit.*

There is no national prejudice in a clear understanding of the Palestinian Covenant. The evidence is too powerful. The gentile is not excluded or an afterthought, nor is the Jew replaced. Regardless of nationality, the New Testament Church is a people belonging to God. The gentile has become a fellowcitizen along *with* the saints of old, as God clearly intended from the beginning.

However, with regard to the Jew-Greek issue, inevitably someone will ask, "But what about Romans 9–11?" Has God abandoned the Jews? Is there still a role for them in the plan of God and in these endtimes? If so, how will they enter in?

Chapter Eleven

All That Call

"...the same Lord over all is rich unto all that call...."

Romans 10:12

Ever since the restoration of the nation of Israel on May 14, 1948 (exactly one year before I was born), the Jews and Israel have remained at the forefront of international attention. I believe that no other nation has generated such extreme responses from such diverse groups worldwide. Some nations have attempted to mobilize against Israel, to bring about her destruction— only to be frustrated by her military, other nations, or even supernatural intervention. Other nations have supported and protected Israel for various political, religious, and economic reasons. Even within America there has been great conflict between people who believe that God is still working on behalf of the natural descendants of Abraham, and those who propagate anti-Semitism through teaching that the gentile Church has completely replaced the Jews in God's affections and promise. Yet the New

Testament clearly speaks to this issue. God's great love for the Jewish people and His predetermined purpose for their end-time restoration, as they accept Jesus Christ as their Messianic Deliverer (Savior), is set forth in three magnificent chapters of the Pauline Epistles—Romans 9–11.

The primary issue here is not one's eschatological position; nor is it any person's slant concerning Israel's national posture in the last days. It was firmly established by Paul through the mind of the Spirit that God would regather and restore the Jewish people. The principal thrust of the apostle's revelation deals rather with *how* the Jews (or men from any nation) are to be saved.

The point is this: Romans 9–11 are contextually soteriological (the Greek word for "salvation" is *soteria*), not eschatological. These three chapters constitute an integral and natural part of the grand biblical theme of God's righteousness by faith alone. Let the apostle speak for himself. In the middle of Romans 9–11, Paul lays down the keynote and recurring theme of these 90 verses.

Rom. 10:12-13, KJV

> *For there is no difference between the Jew and the Greek: for the same Lord over all is rich unto all that call upon Him.*
>
> *For whosoever shall call upon the name of the Lord shall be saved.*

"...all that call...whosoever..."—There is no gender prejudice, no racial prejudice, and now no national prejudice. The righteousness of Christ reduces all men to the point of human depravity. Every person is a sinner in need of a Savior. That he is male or female, black or white, Jew or Greek, matters not. Read this fresh look at Romans 9–11 with an open and ready mind, ever noting the simplicity of the gospel of Jesus Christ to all nations. You may want to have your Bible open to study along as you read the rest of this chapter.

Paul was a great man of prayer and intercession. Although he was sent by God to be the apostle to the "uncircumsion" (the gentiles), he still had a constant burden and desire for the salvation of his own people, the Jews (Rom. 9:1-5). God did not remove Paul's burden; nor did He in any way rebuke or discourage it, as He had Paul's petition for the removal of his "thorn in the flesh" (2 Cor. 12:7-9). Throughout his ministry, Paul experienced great heaviness, or sadness, as well as continual dejection and grief of heart due to this burden. His Epistle to the Romans introduces the initial premise that this Jew-Greek question is a matter of the *heart*, or *spirit*, and not of the letter; each man must experience heart circumcision.

The apostle unceasingly wished and prayed to God that he himself could be "accursed" (or *anathema*) on behalf of his natural kinsmen, or blood relatives. These were his fellow countrymen, Israelites according to the flesh, not the Spirit. He was willing to go to hell if they would be saved. And indeed, there will be a great God-ordained awakening among Abraham's natural descendants. It is righteous and noble for men to have a burden for them, and we must undergird those with a specific evangelistic call to reach the Jewish people. But again, the issue is not and has never been that they *will* be saved, but rather the question has been *how* they will be saved. The basis for their redemption, as with all men, is *faith*, not nationality.

According to Romans 9:4, to the natural Jew belonged the adoption (as they were grafted into God), as did the glory that was in the face of Moses, the covenantal promises of blessing, the giving of the law, their service to God, and the promises of the Messiah who would come and bring the delivering reality to all these shadows.

Paul knew that if anyone should enjoy the benefits of the New Covenant, it should be his people. Through faith in Christ, they could receive their New Testament placement into the Kingdom of God, the greater glory revealed in the face of Jesus, the fulfillment of both the Abrahamic and Davidic Covenants, the receiving of a higher law, the experience of true worship, and direct participation into His divine nature (see Jn. 4:34; Rom. 8:1-4; 2 Cor. 4:6; 2 Pet. 1:3-4).

The promises given to the patriarchal fathers—Abraham, Isaac, and Jacob—were confirmed or secured by Jesus Christ, the legal covenantal Heir of all things (Acts 3:13; Rom. 15:8; Heb. 1:2). The apostle thus gives honor to whom honor is due, for the Messiah came through the Davidic flesh of the Jewish family. Earlier in Romans he gave honor and credit to the Jews for being entrusted with "the very words of God" (Rom. 3:1-2, NIV). A scholar and teacher like the apostle Paul was well aware of his rich Jewish heritage and all that his people represented in the plan of God. Yet he still yearned for them to receive the fullness God had for them through faith in their Messiah, Jesus Christ.

Rom 9:6-8, AMP

*However, it is not as though God's Word had failed
[coming to nothing]. For it is not everybody who is a descendant of Jacob (Israel) who belongs to [the true] Israel.*

*And they are not all the children of Abraham be-
cause they are by blood his descendants. No, [the promise was] Your descendants will be called and counted
through the line of Isaac [though Abraham had an older
son].*

*That is to say, it is not the children of the body [of
Abraham] who are made God's children, but it is the offspring to whom the promise applies that shall be
counted [as Abraham's true] descendants.*

Paul unquestionably shows in Romans 9:6-8 that the
qualification for belonging to the "true Israel" of God
does not rest upon one's nationality. The only seed that
counts with God is that of faith. Isaac was a miracle baby,
born of promise. So the New Testament Christian, regardless of nationality, is born of the Spirit and promise.
The apostolic record is powerfully clear: Those who are
apart from faith are not the children of God. Many Jews
did believe in Paul's day, constituting a remnant according to the election of grace.

Referencing Genesis 18:14 and 25:21-23, the apostle
continues in Romans 9:9-11 to point out that bona fide
salvation is not by works. Every true spiritual reality
comes by promise, and is appropriated by faith. God's
purpose or intention is by election. This divine determination was purposed in Christ Jesus our Lord. God's

holy calling is not according to works but by grace that was given to us in Christ Jesus before the world began. His plan will stand; it will abide. It is of grace, not "works." This word in Romans 9:11 means "toil (as an effort or occupation); by implication, an act." It is rendered in the King James Version as "deed, doing, labour, work." All is "of" Him, denoting origin and character. In Romans 9:12-16, Paul quotes Genesis 25:21-23, Malachi 1:2-3, and Exodus 33:19 to further substantiate His message of God's sovereign mercy, grace, and election.

Rom. 9:17-18, KJV

For the scripture saith unto Pharaoh, Even for this same purpose have I raised thee up, that I might shew My power in thee, and that My name might be declared throughout the earth.

Therefore hath He mercy on whom He will have mercy, and whom He will He hardeneth.

In Romans 9:17-24 the apostle used the example of Pharaoh and the "power" (*dunamis*) or supernatural ability that was manifested in the Exodus. According to His will or desire, God is merciful to some and "hardeneth" others. This latter word in Romans 9:18 means "to render stubborn." No one can resist or stand against His will. No one, regardless of nationality, can contradict or dispute God. He is the divine Potter with "power" or "authority" over the clay. All this is to show and make known the riches of His glory on "vessels of mercy" (Rom. 9:23), whether Jew or Greek, whom He fitted in advance for glory! This one new, "called out" Man, the "us" of Romans 9:24, reiterates the theme of this doctrinal chapter— one Body by the cross.

To accent his point, Paul recites Hosea 1:10 and 2:23 in Romans 9:25-26 (compare 1 Pet. 2:10). This great salvation does not hinge upon one's nationality. He then quotes from Isaiah 10:22-23 in Romans 9:27, who prophesied that a "remnant," or "remainder," of His people shall be saved. Then and now, true deliverance is by the election of grace through faith. It is noteworthy that verse 27 mentions "Israel" in the same context as this new "people" of verses 25-26. God will "finish" or "entirely complete" this work concisely and speedily (Rom. 9:28).

The conclusion of Paul's discussion in Romans 9:30-33 has to do with "the righteousness which is of faith." The "gentiles" have received this grace and have been brought into God's election alongside the Jews of faith. Once again, this word is *ethnos* and denotes firstly, "a multitude or company"; then, "a multitude of people of the same nature or genus, a nation, people." Paul uses *ethnos* elsewhere in Romans 1:5, 3:29, 4:17, and 16:25-26 as he proclaims that salvation in Christ is void of national prejudice.

The Old Testament nation ardently pursued the righteousness of the law. They did not "attain" or "arrive at" that goal because they sought it by works and not faith. The "stumblingstone" or "rock of offense" in Romans 9:32 is Jesus Christ Himself (Is. 28:16; 1 Pet. 2:6-8). His finished work on the cross causes men from all nations to stub their religious toe (their walk in tradition) as they trip over the singleness and simplicity that is in Christ.

Rom. 9:33b, KJV

> ...*and whosoever believeth on Him shall not be ashamed.*

The main point of Romans 9 is that God is calling out a people to Himself. He began with Abraham, who was credited righteous due to his faith, and symbolized for us the heritage that is ours by faith. This election and grace of God belongs to *whosoever* believes in Jesus Christ. No person of faith (regardless of gender, race, or nationality) shall be put to shame.

When the Jews are grafted in again, it will be by the blood of Christ, not by the blood of bulls and goats that could never take away sin (Rom. 11:23-26; Heb. 9:13-14; 10:4). That is why God is currently raising up key ministries to carry a special burden for the Jewish people (just as He is mandating others to sow in other parts of His glorious end-time harvest). God has not abandoned the Jews. He is preparing to open a whole new chapter in their experience as the flames of revival begin to sweep around the world. The burden Paul and others have carried for the salvation of the Jews has not been forgotten or overlooked. They will not be missed in God's great harvest.

The Word of Faith

Romans 10 continues Paul's theme of faith and grace. Remember, these three chapters are soteriological, not eschatological—they primarily deal with the basis of salvation for the whole creation, showing that God was in Christ reconciling the *world* unto Himself.

The first five verses of chapter 10 describe some of Paul's natural brethren who (like many Christians today) minded earthly things. They had a zeal for God without "knowledge." This word in Romans 10:2 is *epignosis* and means "recognition, (by implication) full discernment, acknowledgment"— full and accurate knowledge. (Remember that *prejudice* means to "pre-judge" without having all the facts.)

Romans 10:3 provides us with a Bible definition for "religion." "Ignorant" means "not to know (through lack of information or intelligence); by implication, to ignore (through disinclination)." Such persons go about attempting to establish their own righteousness by teaching that the righteousness of God has natural criteria (either by natural birth or by works). They refuse to submit themselves to the Word of God.

Romans 10:4 definitively states: "Christ is the end of the law." The Last Adam brought a lasting end to the consequences of the first Adam's sin. Jesus' finished work demolished all national prejudice. The law was partial, for it only ministered to one nation (or denomination or imagi-nation [doctrine]). God desired to raise up a greater priesthood. Therefore, Levi was superseded by Melchisedec. The priesthood has changed. Jesus was the end of the law, fulfilling Moses (see Jn. 1:17; 2 Cor. 3:13; 1 Tim. 1:5; Heb. 7:12).

"To *every one* that believeth...." Verse 4 trumpets the sound of grace once again. The only condition to be met is faith, not the righteousness which is by the law.

Paul's notable words regarding the word of faith in Romans 10:6-10 are taken from Deuteronomy 29:11-14 and the Palestinian Covenant (discussed in Chapter 10 of this book).

By the work of the Spirit, this word of faith is near every believer, and is found in two places: his heart and his mouth. If faith is only in his heart but not his mouth, he walks in silent faith. If faith is in his mouth but not his heart, he will speak only empty words (presumption).

Real New Testament faith is imputed and imparted. It is a gift, a living reality. Romans 10:9-10 has been memorized and used by soul-winners for years to explain the simplicity of being born again. These verses apply to *all* men, to Jew and Greek. The word for "confess" in verse 9 is *homologeo* and means "to assent, covenant, acknowledge." It literally means "to speak the same thing," and it has to do with making covenant with God, not based on the politics of any nation, gender, or race, but on the saving grace of Jesus Christ.

Rom. 10:11-13, KJV

For the scripture saith, Whosoever believeth on Him shall not be ashamed.

For there is no difference between the Jew and the Greek: for the same Lord over all is rich unto all that call upon Him.

For whosoever shall call upon the name of the Lord shall be saved.

Quoting Isaiah 28:16, Paul repeats himself. Are you getting his point? Whosoever believes "on" Him— this preposition *epi* describes our leaning "upon" Jesus in full dependence. Whosoever shall believe on Him shall not be ashamed or disgraced, and whosoever shall call upon the name of the Lord shall be saved (Rom. 5:5; 9:33)!

There is no "difference" between the Jew and the Greek; all may call upon the Lord! This word in Romans 10:12 is *diastole* and means "a variation, distinction." I beseech you to hear Paul's apostolic proclamation (compare Rom. 3:22-23).

Jesus is the "same Lord" over *all* men, and is "rich" unto *all* that call upon Him. There is no difference! In Christ, God's covenant blessings are available to every person. Christ's work opened the door for the gentiles to enter in by grace. "All that call" are recipients and benefactors of the wealth of the New Covenant, the commonwealth of Israel. Paul spoke elsewhere of these "riches" (see Rom. 2:4; 9:23; 11:33; Eph. 1:7,18; 2:7; 3:8,16; Phil. 4:19; Col. 1:27; 2:2). Jesus Christ experienced our poverty in His incarnation that we might be made rich in His exaltation. Paul clearly states that these riches are for "all that call." In other words, if you don't call, you stay poor!

Romans 10:14-17 next sets forth God's apostolic plan and method to proclaim this good news to all the world (Is. 52:7; 53:1). Not all have "obeyed" the gospel; not all Jews, nor all gentiles. This word in Romans 10:16 is *hupakouo*, and it means "to hear under (as a subordinate), to listen attentively; by implication, to heed or conform to a command or authority." Men from every nation are commanded to hear the words of King Jesus.

Romans 10:18-21 testifies that the Jewish nation heard the word of the gospel proclaimed by the early Church but did not believe. The Sanhedrin's stoning of Stephen in Acts 7 marked the complete Jewish renunciation of their Messiah. In Acts 8–10, Philip ministered to the Ethiopian eunuch, and God called Peter, the apostle to the circumcision, to share the gospel of Jesus Christ with the gentiles. As a result, the Holy Ghost was poured out upon Cornelius' household. Later, through Paul, God turned to all the nations. The gospel was then uttered to all men and covered the earth.

The apostle finished Romans 10 by quoting Deuteronomy 32:21 and Isaiah 65:1-2.

Rom. 10:21, KJV

> *But to Israel He saith, All day long I have stretched forth My hands unto a disobedient and gainsaying people.*

The mercy of God, which is rich to all men, continued to reach out to the Jewish people despite their disobedience. His love is patient, even though men are "disobedient" or "willfully unbelieving." The word used for "disobedient" in Romans 10:21 is *apeithes,* and it literally means "no faith" or "without faith." Men and women who refuse Jesus Christ are also "gainsaying" or "unpersuadable." This word is *antilego,* and it literally means that which is spoken "against or instead of the word"— the traditions of men.

To summarize Romans 9 and 10, Paul has made no difference between Jew or Greek in coming to God. Both must come to God by *faith* through hearing the Word of God. In no way did the apostle Paul argue for the preferential treatment of one nation over another in the Church, nor did he permit the entertainment of any prejudicial or exclusionary notion.

The Good Olive Tree Is Jesus

Paul begins Romans 11 by affirming that God has not "cast away" the Jews. Israel's response to their Messiah and the early Church did not cause God to reject them or forget His people. Just as Elijah received God's "answer" that he was not alone in his obedience and faith in the living God, Paul, too, was assured of a remnant among his countrymen. This word in Romans 11:4 is *chrematismos* and means "a divine response or revelation, an oracle." Similarly, a clear understanding of Romans 9–11 can only come by the revelation of the Spirit. In Elijah's and Paul's day, Jehovah had reserved "unto Himself" a righteous remnant. It was a remnant that was elected by the grace of God. Yet Paul's burden for the rest of his countrymen remained.

Romans 11:6 explains that the righteousness that is by faith is the product of New Testament grace, not Old Testament works (compare Rom. 3:27-28; 4:2,6; Gal. 2:16; 3:10). A man is not justified by the works of the law, but by the faith of Jesus Christ. Those whose salvation is based upon the works of the law are still under its penalty.

The apostle continues in Romans 11:7-12 to show that no one apart from faith can obtain or attain the righteousness of God. The Jews of Paul's time who believed in Christ had become partakers of the divine nature, but those who refused their Messiah were, like Pharaoh in Romans 9:17-18, still blinded and hardened through unbelief. Paul recognized this as a temporary blindness and pressed on in faith and hope in the promised restoration. The New International Version of Romans 11:11 declares that the Jewish people did not stumble and "fall beyond recovery"!

Paul also quotes Isaiah 6:9-10, 29:10, and Psalm 69:22-23 to further support his discourse. Any man who refuses Christ remains in a state of spiritual "slumber" or "stupor, lethargy." The eyes of such a one's understanding is "darkened," his perceptions "obscured." Yet the same God who allowed their eyes to become darkened is well able to open them so that His glory may be revealed (Jn. 9:1-7)!

Rom. 11:11-13, TLB

Does this mean that God has rejected His Jewish people forever? Of course not! His purpose was to make His salvation available to the Gentiles, and then the Jews would be jealous and begin to want God's salvation for themselves.

Now if the whole world became rich as a result of God's offer of salvation, when the Jews stumbled over it and turned it down, think how much greater a blessing the world will share in later on when the Jews, too, come to Christ.

The Book of Acts tells the story of the fall of Judaism and the rise of Christianity. Through their "fall" the gospel came to every nation in order that the Jews might be provoked to jealousy and also be brought into faith. Romans 11:11-12 establishes a powerful scriptural base for evangelizing the Jewish people. They have not fallen so far that they cannot recover. Their transgression meant riches for the world, and their loss, riches for the nations, but God's redemptive plan has far greater than that in store for Jew and gentile. In Christ, the fullness of the Jews will be restored through grace and faith.

In Romans 11:13-15, Paul makes plain the purpose of his writing Romans 9–11. Even as he fulfilled his calling to the gentiles, Paul desired that God's work through him among the gentiles would help to usher even more of his natural countrymen into faith and salvation. A Jewish man or woman, as anyone else, can be saved by exercising faith in the finished work of Jesus Christ. The shed blood of Jesus, the perfect sacrificial Lamb, is our common ground for justification by faith. Through the blood of Jesus there is no distinction regarding gender, race, or nation; His blood brings us into unity through His righteousness by faith.

The apostle prayed that he might "provoke to emulation [jealousy]" or "excite to rivalry" his kinsmen according to the flesh. Their rejection of Messiah resulted in the reconciling of all nations to God in Christ. But God has purposed to receive and accept them as well through the blood of His beloved Son, and raise them up from spiritual death (Jn. 5:24; Rom. 6:1-14; Eph. 2:1). Again, Paul's theme never questions that they can and will be saved; rather, it has to do with the basis of their salvation and standing in true righteousness before God.

Paul uses the symbol of the olive tree to further illustrate his message. The truths of this crucial Bible chapter are unlocked by understanding that the "good olive tree" of Romans 11:24 is Jesus, the "true vine," the "tree of life" (Gen. 3:24; Jn. 15:1; Rev. 22:2)! Moreover, the good olive tree of Romans 11:24 is also the tree of *faith*, depicting our new nature in Christ. The olive branches that are wild by nature were once part of the tree of unbelief, and represent the untamed Adamic or Ishmael nature (see Rom. 11:17,24; Eph. 2:1-3; 4:22-24).

The fruit and blessing of the branches of an olive tree are not a result of the strength and work of the branch, for it is the root that supplies the riches and blessing. In this passage, we see that the branches of faith receive their strength and nourishment from the greatest Root of all, the true Vine, the living Word, Jesus Christ.

These next nine verses of Romans 11 are most essential to fully understand the chapter as a whole. Many teach that the "good olive tree" is the physical nation of Israel and that the "wild olive tree" represents the "gentile" nations. But Romans 11:16-24 reveals that *Jesus* is:

1. The holy "firstfruits" (Rom. 11:16; see also Rom. 8:29; 1 Cor. 15:20,23; Col. 1:15,18).

2. The "root" (Rom. 11:16; see also Rom. 15:12; Rev. 5:5; 22:16).

3. The fat (anointed) "olive tree" (Rom. 11:17; see also Lk. 4:18; Acts 4:27; 10:38; Heb. 1:9).

4. The standing Tree of "faith" (Rom. 11:20; see also Acts 7:55; Rev. 5:6; 14:1).

5. The abiding "goodness" ("kindness") of God (Rom. 11:22; see also Rom. 2:4; Eph. 2:7; Tit. 3:4).

6. National Israel's "own olive tree" (because He was born of David's seed) (Rom. 11:24; see also Rom. 1:3; 9:5; 2 Tim. 2:8).

Jesus declared Himself to be the true Vine. To be "in Christ" is to abide in His own life. Jesus is holy; therefore, the whole "lump" of dough, whether Jew or Greek, is holy (Rom. 11:16). Paul affirmed to the Corinthians that "we being many are one bread, and one body: for we are all partakers of that one bread" (1 Cor. 10:17). Believers are in union with Him. As He is, so are we (1 Jn. 4:17). His life is our only source of life.

Romans 1:17 attests that God's redemptive purposes were sent "to the Jew first," and then "also to the Greek." Daniel had predicted that Messiah would confirm Jeremiah's New Covenant (Jer. 31:31-34; Dan. 9:27) with many of the prophet's own people (the Jews). And Jesus' earthly ministry displayed an obvious emphasis on bringing His Kingdom to the Jews. He did not exclude the gentiles from receiving from Him, but He made the focus of His earthly ministry clear. Once again, we see that the gentiles who received from Him did so according to their faith (Mt. 15:22-28). Even after the crucifixion and resurrection, Jesus' parting words instructed His followers to minister the gospel first to the Jews and then throughout the world to all nations (Mt. 28:19-20; Acts 1:8).

The Old Testament prophets repeatedly warned God's people about idolatry, else He would root them out of the land (see Deut. 29:28; 1 Kings 14:15; Ps. 52:5; Is. 40:24; Jer. 1:10; Mal. 4:1; Mt. 3:7-12). Romans 11:17-23 show how the warnings of the prophets became fulfilled due to their unbelief. The "wild" olive tree of Romans 11:17 represents the "wild" Adamic nature or Ishmael nature (Gen. 16:12; Dan. 5:21), regardless of fleshly nationality. We weren't "born to be wild"—we were all *born "wild"*! This is the Greek word *agrios* and means "wild (as pertaining to the country), literally (natural) or figuratively (fierce)." It speaks of that which grows "wild" in the field—the beast nature. Jesus taught in Matthew 13:38 that the field is the world. To be wild is to be worldly.

One born wild in Adam who receives Jesus as his personal Savior becomes engrafted into Christ to be a co-participant of His "fatness" or "richness, oiliness." Oil is the biblical symbol for the anointing of the Holy Spirit. Those in union with the true Vine share His anointing! We become privileged partakers of His Word (the root) and His Spirit (the fatness).

Romans 11:17-23 can also serve as a strong warning to us today. Paul warns us Greeks to guard our pride. God did not "spare" or "treat leniently" His Old Testament people. We have no room for arrogance toward those who were broken off due to unbelief. For those who were broken off can be grafted back in by the same means we were brought in—by faith. Our "boast" or "glorying, rejoicing" can only be in Christ, the divine Root who sustains and carries us. He alone is our Rock, our support and stay. All things consist or are held together by Him. Men are broken off from the Vine by unbelief. But in Christ alone do we stand by faith. Let us not become proud and conceited, but maintain our reverential fear of the Lord. God's severity or goodness does not hinge upon one's gender, race, or nationality—the key is to continue, or abide, in Christ!

The Greek word for "unbelief" in Romans 11:20 is *apaistia* and means "faithlessness, disbelief." It is a combination of the negative particle "a" and the word for "faith"—"no faith." All of Romans 9–11 continues to rise and fall on this one central idea: Right standing with God is by faith alone, regardless of one's nationality. Without faith, it is impossible to please God.

Rom. 11:23, AMP

And even those others [the fallen branches, Jews], if they do not persist in [clinging to] their unbelief, will be grafted in, for God has the power to graft them in again.

This verse is crucial. If any person from any background will renounce his sin of unbelief and come to God through the blood of His divine Son, mankind's Passover Lamb, he will be grafted into the true, New Covenant Vine. With regard to the Jewish people, God intends to graft them in "again." This is the Greek word *palin* and means "(adverbially) anew, (of place) back, (of time) once more, or (conjunctionally) furthermore or on the other hand." It is used with reference to repeated action or in the sense of "further" or "moreover."

God will save the Jews! He has a "further" purpose: their salvation! Joel 2:28-32 had prophesied that God would pour out His Spirit upon *all* flesh, and that *whosoever* would call upon the name of the Lord would be saved. The great outpouring of the Holy Ghost on the Day of Pentecost was only a small part of all that Joel had predicted. The word for "pour out of" used in Acts 2:17, when Peter referred to this important prophetic passage, is *ekcheo* (from *ek*, meaning "out of," and *cheo*, meaning "to pour"). This was but the Pentecostal earnest and firstfruits of the present end-time Feast of Tabernacles!

That which took place in the upper room and the streets of Jerusalem in Acts 2 was "the former rain moderately." In the latter part of this age, Joel 2:23 promises that God will cause "the former, and the latter rain" to come down together! The devout ingathering of 3,000 Jews that glorious day of Pentecost (Acts 2:5-11; Rom. 11:5) was but a miniature picture of the move of God that we anticipate among them in the days to come!

God is "able" to graft them in again. This word in verse 23 is *dunatos* and means "powerful or capable." It is in the same word family as *dunamis* and the root word *dunamai*, and speaks of the regenerating, resurrection power of the Holy Spirit. By His Spirit, God desires to bring this people, along with all nations, back into the household of faith.

The apostle adds in Romans 11:24 (echoed in Ephesians 2:3) that we were all wild "by nature." There are but two kinds of men on this planet, Christ and Adam. These depict two natures: beauty and the beast. There were only two trees in the Garden and two trees in Romans 11—the Tree of life (the good olive Tree) and the tree of the knowledge of good and evil (the wild olive tree). According to His divine plan from the beginning of creation, those who receive Christ are grafted back into God "contrary to nature"—it is a supernatural work wrought of and by the Spirit.

Paul exhorts us to evangelize the Jewish people regarding the gospel of Jesus Christ, for how "much more" readily should they come to the One who is their "own" olive Tree (Rom. 11:24). The essence of the New Testament blessing is "much more" (as in Rom. 5:9-20; 2 Cor. 3:9-11; Heb. 9:14).

John 1:11 says that at the beginning of this age Jesus came unto His "own," but His "own" received Him not. The closing verses of Romans 11 prophesy that at the end of this age, the Jewish people will bow their knee and make blood covenant with their "own," rightful Messiah!

Again, it is not a question that the Jews will be saved, but rather that they, through saving faith in Jesus Christ, will be grafted back into His ongoing Messianic Body, one holy nation made up of both Jew and Greek— the people of faith from the patriarchs to the present and into eternity! Paul expounded upon the condition of Israel to *prevent* ungodly "conceits," imaginations, and speculations:

Rom. 11:25, KJV

For I would not, brethren, that ye should be ignorant of this mystery, lest ye should be wise in your own conceits; that blindness in part is happened to Israel, until the fulness of the Gentiles be come in.

"Blindness" or "hardness" in part has happened to Israel. This is the Greek word *porosis* and means "stupidity or callousness." It primarily means "a covering with a callus," and it is taken from *poros*, which means "a kind of stone." *Porosis* is a metaphorical description of dulled spiritual perception. It was used by Jesus and Paul to describe the hearts of men. This blindness of the Jews has only been "in part" because although some have rejected the Messiah, others have accepted Jesus Christ. This blindness upon the Jewish people is temporary ("until"), not permanent. What a promise! What hope!

This blindness of the nation as a whole is until "the fulness of the gentiles" takes place. Thayer's Lexicon says, "until the full number of the ingathering of the gentiles has come in."[1] This phrase, "the fullness of the gentiles," has been used in a negative context. Men teach that when the last sinner to make up the Body of Christ is saved, the so-called rapture of the Church will take place. Then, they say, God will renew His program with His chosen people, the Jews.

What was Paul really saying? The Greek word for "fullness" in Romans 11:25 is *pleroma* and means "repletion or completion, (subjectively) what fills (as contents, supplement, copiousness, multitude), or (objectively) what is filled (as container, performance, period)." It is rendered in the King James Version as "which is put in to fill up, piece that filled up, fulfilling, full, fulness."

This Pauline phrase is positive, not negative. The "fulness of the gentiles" speaks of a time when the Body of Christ throughout all the nations comes to the "fulness" of His stature! As set forth in Ephesians 4:8-15, the purpose of the present reign of Christ is to fill all things. The full measure of His Manhood takes place as all the nations come into His Kingdom. Paul said it this way:

Eph. 4:13, AMP

[That it might develop] until we all attain oneness in the faith and in the comprehension of the [full and accurate] knowledge of the Son of God, that [we might arrive] at really mature manhood (the completeness of personality which is nothing less than the standard height of Christ's own perfection), the measure of the

stature of the fullness of the Christ and the completeness found in Him.

Simply stated, "the fulness of the gentiles" is the fulfillment of the Great Commission of King Jesus, the greatest Son of David, to take His gospel to every creature and nation (Mt. 28:18-20; Mk. 16:15-20; Acts 1:8)!

This may seem outrageous to consider, but when the Jewish people hear the saints from every nation (including the Arab nations) speaking with other tongues and see them working miracles in the mighty name of Jesus, they will be provoked to jealousy and return to their Messiah!

> "Yes, Israel fell. But Israel will recover! Yes, Israel was disobedient and obstinate. But Israel will receive a new heart! The Redeemer will 'turn ungodliness away from Jacob.' He will 'take away their sins.' This people that has received more than its share of suffering will be blessed in its final end. It's time for the blessing to come! How great is the wisdom of God."[2]

The destruction of Jerusalem was the sign on the earth that the Jewish mission as a witness from among the nations had ended and the gentile mission to all nations had begun. This international objective of God's Messianic Kingdom would be a successful one. Jesus knew that the promises of the Old Testament prophets predicted the triumph of His New Testament gospel. Just as natural Israel was called to answer for their response to the gospel of the Kingdom, so would every nation. The Lord told His disciples on the Mount of Olives:

Lk. 21:24, KJV

...and Jerusalem shall be trodden down of the Gentiles, until the times of the Gentiles be fulfilled.

The destruction of Jerusalem would serve as a warning to all nations throughout the gentile mission. Just as Israel could not escape the judgment of God, neither can any other nation. However, in the fulfilling of the Great Commission, there remained a promise, a hope for Israel. The Lord's followers were being sent first to the Jew, and then to the gentile. Even in this Olivet discourse, the Lord used the time-related word "until"—Jerusalem would be trampled "until" the global mission is successfully completed, "until" the nations become filled with the glory of God. God has not rejected Israel or the Jews. We cannot overlook either His commission or His promise.

The apostle Paul affirms these truths in his Epistle to the Romans. This hardness of heart will be removed. According to the plan and purpose of God, the Jewish people will be provoked to jealousy by the blessings of the Kingdom coming upon all the other nations. When Israel sees those nations walking in the light of the Messiah, fully enjoying the covenantal blessings of the Kingdom of God as adopted heirs of God in Christ Jesus, they will repent and be grafted back into the people of God!

Rom. 11:26, KJV

And so all Israel shall be saved....

How one grasps and views the ultimate scope of this awesome declaration is not the point. It is not the aim of this book to emphasize personal points of preference or differences of interpretation and eschatology. My desire is to emphasize the biblical basis for our unity in Christ with persons of every gender, race, and nation. Through God's grace and through faith in the completed work of Jesus Christ, gentile believers, regardless of nation or natural culture, are full brothers in faith with our Jewish brethren. Neither Jew nor gentile can overlook or omit the promises of God to the natural descendants of Abraham, or His desire that they all be circumcised in their hearts as they receive by faith their own true Messiah. I have not fully fathomed the answers to some of the questions raised by these passages. Yet, we have clearly seen through the words of Paul and other Scriptures that Israel shall be saved. This salvation is not open to question. And as I have emphasized repeatedly, Paul's objective in these crucial chapters is to indicate the way his kinsmen (and how men and women of every nation) are to come to God.

This observation may help us to better understand Paul's words here. "And all Israel shall 'be saved' ": Paul used this same phrase earlier in this Epistle (Rom. 9:27; 10:1,9,13). Salvation is by grace and faith. Quoting the Old Testament prophet, Paul goes on to affirm in Romans 11:26 that there is only *one* "Deliverer," or "Savior." (Isaiah 59:20 calls Him the "Redeemer.") That He comes out of Zion identifies this deliverer as Jesus, as the Messiah, the rightful King and Son of David (see Mt. 1:21; Lk. 1:31-33; Acts 4:12; Gal. 3:13-14).

Isaiah 59:20 says that this Redeemer shall come unto "them that turn from transgression in Jacob." This again describes a Jewish remnant, according to the election of grace, who recognize and receive their Messiah. It also reveals that Jesus alone can deliver men from the "ungodliness" or "impiety" of the Jacob nature, the sinful Adamic nature. It is the power of God, illustrated through the work of Jesus, that transforms a "supplanter" into "Israel," one who rules with authority, blessing, and power. On Calvary's cross, Jesus cut the New "Covenant" and did what the blood of bulls and goats could never do (Heb. 9:13-14; 10:4). He took away the sins of His people, including the sins of all people of all nations who would come to Him by faith (Dan. 9:27; Rom. 11:27; see also Is. 59:21; Jn. 1:29; Acts 1–7). It is by the completed work of Jesus that every believer is blessed with every spiritual blessing in Christ (Eph. 1:3).

As we move further and further into the Day of the Lord and to the fulfillment of Ephesians 4:13 and the international feast of tabernacles, there will be an ever-increasing outpouring of the Holy Spirit upon the Jewish people. God will open their eyes to their need of the Savior, and they will come to Him, taking their rightful place among the people of God. At the beginning of this age, the Jews rejected their Messiah. At the close of this age, they shall gladly receive Him and enter into the fullness of blessing that was promised in ages past!

Again, I praise God for all those with a genuine burden for the nation of Israel. Be encouraged, brethren, for the prophetic season is upon us when the Jewish people will be grafted back again into the true Vine, the "good olive tree." The season has come for them to join the ranks of His whole Messianic Body, His glorious Church made up of both Jew and Greek!

Paul acknowledged in Romans 11:28-32 that those who had rejected their Messiah were enemies, or adversaries, with regard to the gospel—like all those who reject Jesus. However, because of the promises made to the fathers—Abraham, Isaac, and Jacob—they, and all sinners, were loved because of the election of grace (Rom. 11:28; see also Is. 53:6; Rom. 5:8; 1 Tim. 1:16). First Peter 3:18 declares that Jesus died, "the just for the unjust, that He might bring us [both Jew and Greek] to God...."

Rom. 11:29, KJV

For the gifts and calling of God are without repentance.

The "gifts" (the charismata) and "the calling" (there is the definite article "the") of God are "without repentance"— they are *irrevocable*. God has not cast away or in any way revoked or nullified His promises to Israel or the Jews. The entering of gentile believers into the heritage of faith did not supplant or replace God's word to them, as this chapter has clearly shown. However, Romans 11:29 is not limited to the Jewish people alone. Indeed, God has a foreordained purpose for every nation and man to be realized within the context of a relationship with Him and through the Body of Christ. Each man's calling is by faith and promise. There is but one Body, and one Spirit, as we (both Jew and Greek) have been called in one hope of our calling (Eph. 4:4).

These verses put both Jew and Greek on the same footing in Christ. Both must believe and receive the mercy of God. God has "concluded" all men in unbelief that He might offer the gospel of Jesus Christ without national distinction and have mercy on all men of all nations—Jew and Greek. This word in Romans 11:32 is *sugkleio* and means "to shut together; to include or embrace in a common subjection to." It is used in Luke 5:6 to describe a great catch of fish, and by the apostle in Galatians 3:22 to declare that "...the scripture hath concluded all under sin...." Let every evangelist arise! Make ready your nets. It's time for the catch!

Rom. 11:32, NIV

> *For God has bound all men over to disobedience so that He may have mercy on them all.*

There was absolutely no national prejudice in the mind and mouth of Paul when he penned Romans 9–11. The literary apostle was overwhelmed by the wisdom of God and closed out Romans 11:33-36 in one grand, crescendo of worship as he quoted Isaiah 40:13-14!

Rom. 11:36, AMP

> *For from Him and through Him and to Him are all things. [For all things originate with Him and come from Him; all things live through Him, and all things center in and tend to consummate and to end in Him.] To Him be glory forever! Amen (so be it).*

Do you know who you are (in Christ)? Do you know what you have? Do you know how to get it? Are you walking in unity and love with your brothers and sisters in Christ Jesus? Are you seeking to respect the differences and giftings of others within the Body, while focusing on the things that bring unity and fellowship rather than division? Divisions based on gender, race, and nationality (whether natural or conceptual—physical countries as well as denomi-nations and imagi-nations) will always separate and divide.

Jewish believer, are you accepting your gentile brothers and sisters and allowing God to express His nature through them? I encourage you to re-examine your special heritage as a nation of faith and note the many "strangers" that God brought within the camps of Israel to bless His people and to provide examples of His power and might. Consider the fathers of faith before Abraham and other gentiles who came after, who played great roles in the purposes and plan of God. Experience the full wealth of your heritage through a fresh understanding of the grand scope of God's plan and design. I encourage you to allow love and forgiveness to permeate your relations with your brothers and sisters of all nations who are in Christ.

Gentile believer, are you recognizing your shared heritage of faith and walking in understanding and appreciation of your Jewish brothers and sisters? Have you appreciated the many ways you have benefited from the sacrifices and gifts of the Jewish fathers? Remember that it is through Israel and the Jewish people that the very words of God were communicated to man— even the written Word of God through which we, too, have heard and come to faith. It is through the people of Israel and the fathers of faith that we have received the many examples, symbols, and types through which we have obtained our own understanding of the heart and workings of God. It is through the nation of Israel that God chose to send the Messiah. It was due to God's provision for us that the hearts of that nation were hardened and salvation was extended to all nations, including the descendants of Israel. Volumes could be written on the ways the Jews have contributed to our culture, our faith, and our history. The words of the apostles, as well as those of Jesus Himself, show God's great desire for this people to know Him in all His fullness; therefore, I encourage you to pray for God's Spirit to move among them and to usher in God's promised restoration through faith. Encourage those who carry a clear burden for this people, and walk in love with your brothers and sisters in Christ of every nation and culture.

Christian, are you also allowing God's presence and power to flow freely through both Jew and Greek (and others who may be culturally or theologically different than yourself) as His Spirit moves and is made manifest among them through the grace and work of Jesus Christ? Jesus did not come to abolish anyone's culture. He did not come to destroy the creative personal preference or expression that He has given each nation. He came to make Himself known and to make His salvation available to all peoples, regardless of their origin! He desires for His Body to express His heart, mind, and life—not man's. God's Spirit clearly is calling each one of us to tear down every wall that divides so that Jesus Christ, our King and Deliverer, will be lifted up and glorified!

The three prejudices—gender, racial, and national—must be cut away from the words and actions of God's people. These walls must come down! We have carefully examined each of them, biblically and historically. It is through Jesus' blood that we have all become part of His Body and His purpose in this earth. The Body of Christ is His glorious Church, made up of male and female, one Race from among the races, one holy Nation, a people belonging to God!

The "hope of glory" mentioned in Colossians 1:27 is God's own hope! The divine anticipation is a vast anointed family of sons and daughters in the image of the Pattern Son—"Christ in and among all of you"—Christ fully formed in a people.

We began by uncovering the root of all prejudice: man's greatest fear—rejection. But God has not rejected man or woman. He has not rejected black, white, nor any other race. He has not rejected Jew or Greek. But He has created and formed each and is at work within each to perform His will for His good pleasure (Eph. 1:5,9; Phil. 2:13). God loves each, and from the foundations of the world He has planned and made provision for each to be restored and enter into the blessing, provision, and righteousness of His Kingdom. We have no right to fear, exclude, or reject what God has made accepted in the beloved; for through the blood of Jesus we are all gathered together in Christ (Eph. 1:3-10)!

Let us conclude the matter by proclaiming that God's greatest hope is His anointed family; and as we, as one Body, fully enter into the perfecting, completed work of Christ, I boldly prophesy that He shall see His Seed!

Chapter Twelve

God's Greatest Hope: His Anointed Family

"...He shall see His seed...."

Isaiah 53:10

Chapter One of this writing presented Christ, the new creation Man, the One who transcends every bias and form of bigotry.

Chapter Two divulged that mankind's greatest fear is rejection, the root cause of all human prejudice. The only cure for Adam's predicament is to be forgiven, accepted in the Beloved.

Chapters Three through Six dealt with gender prejudice—the man-woman issue.

Chapters Seven through Nine tackled racial prejudice, biblically and historically.

Chapters Ten and Eleven ventured where few have dared to go; they addressed the purpose and plan of God that includes both Jew and gentile. God wants all men of every nation, culture, and tradition to approach Him by faith and live in unity with one another through Jesus Christ.

Before us is the conclusion of the matter. God's greatest hope is that He shall see His anointed family, His seed, Christ fully formed in one body by the Spirit!

Is. 53:10, KJV

Yet it pleased the Lord to bruise Him; He hath put Him to grief: when Thou shalt make His soul an offering for sin, He shall see His seed, He shall prolong His days, and the pleasure of the Lord shall prosper in His hand.

This verse is profound. Transcending earthly intellect and understanding, it powerfully establishes the divine plan and purpose.

First, Jesus came to this earth as the Son and Seed of the Father. Every Old Testament redemptive name (the "Jehovah" names) of the Father was consummated in the Son. The Father saw His seed, and Jesus prolonged His days, being the full expression of the name and nature of God. Jesus was the Word made flesh, the fullness of the Godhead bodily.

Second, the phrase "He shall see His seed" also refers to Jesus Himself. He (Jesus) shall see His seed (the Church), and "He" (the new creation Man, the corporate, many-membered Body of Christ) shall prolong and extend the ministry of their King into all the earth!

Jesus had no earthly or natural seed. As exampled by the Abrahamic Covenant, the only thing that counts with God is a people of faith, a spiritual seed. The only things worth passing on to the next generations are those eternal things of and by the *Spirit*! Issues pertaining to sex, race, or nationality are but chaff— they are meaningless, belonging to the lower realms of death and dust that are passing away.

Jesus has a generation, a supernatural offspring. The New Testament, Matthew's Gospel in particular, explains:

Mt. 1:1, KJV

The book of the generation of Jesus Christ, the son of David, the son of Abraham.

In its consummate sense, the "book" of the generation of Jesus Christ is a people, the Lamb's book of life. A Messianic people with His divine genes is "of the generation of Jesus Christ." This mood is genitive, denoting origin and character.

"Generation" is singular— one spiritual generation in contrast with the many earthy "generations" of the first Adam— a heavenly people who have been produced from the character of the last Adam, having been made partakers of the divine nature (Gen. 5:1; 1 Cor. 15:44-49; 2 Pet. 1:4). The word *generation* is commonly used with reference to time, but it essentially speaks about something being born and coming forth (with reference to nature).

The generation of Jesus Christ is a people who have been birthed out of Him! We are the offspring of God, His anointed family. Adam was the federal head of a natural race. Jesus is the federal Head of a spiritual people who have been regenerated or born from above.

Isaiah prophesied that Messiah would "see His seed" and that they would "prolong His days." The story of the New Testament Church in the Book of Acts is described by its author Luke in Acts 1:1 as a ministry that continued "...all that Jesus began both to do and teach."

Mt. 1:16-17, KJV

> *And Jacob begat Joseph the husband of Mary, of whom was born Jesus, who is called Christ.*
>
> *So all the generations from Abraham to David are fourteen generations; and from David until the carrying away into Babylon are fourteen generations; and from the carrying away into Babylon unto Christ are fourteen generations.*

The legal Messianic genealogy of Matthew 1:1-17 contains a total of 42 generations. From Abraham to David are 14 generations. From David until the Babylonian captivity are 14 generations. From the Babylonian captivity "unto Christ" are 14 generations.

However, in Matthew 1:12b-17, there appears to be a contradiction. Jechonias was the twenty-eighth generation; following him are Salatheil down to Joseph, the husband of Mary, the fortieth, and Jesus, who is called Christ, the forty-first. Count them again. There is a missing generation. Where is the forty-second generation? Jesus had no earthly seed. Where is His generation? Who is the forty-second generation?

The answer is simple, found in the Greek phrase "unto Christ" or "until Christ." This aligns with Paul's apostolic burden in Galatians 4:19: "...until Christ be formed..." in a people, until the Messiah shows up in His anointed family.

The forty-second "generation" is the Church, the Body of "Christ"! The biblical number denoting man is six. The number seven speaks of perfection. Forty-two is six times seven— the "perfect" man of First Corinthians 13:10-11 (where the key word is "when") and Ephesians 4:13 (where the key word is "till"). The forty-second generation is a mature, many-membered Man, the corporate Messiah, God's anointed Family.

There is one family of God, one Body, and one Head of the Church. One anointed Head (Jesus Christ) with one anointed Body (of Christ) equals one new Man— Christ, the anointed One! To reiterate, Christ, in the fullest sense, is not an individual...He is corporate. The secret of the anointing, the real power of the Holy Spirit, is to be found in His people, His seed, which is comprised of both men and women from every race and nationality!

Who Shall Declare His Generation?

Jesus had no natural children. His seed is spiritual, a people begotten by the Word and Spirit of God (Jn. 3:1-8; Jas. 1:18; 1 Pet. 1:23). The first Adam is no longer our father. Male or female, regardless of race or nationality, we are spirit beings of whom God Almighty is the Father.

Isaiah 53:8a asks, "...and who shall declare His generation?" Psalm 22:30 adds, "A seed shall serve Him; it shall be accounted to the Lord for a generation."

Jesus will realize the spiritual seed who shall prolong His days. This "en-Christed" seed is an anointed army of servants, the forty-second generation, the glorious, end-time Church marked by righteousness, prayer, and praise. Jesus is the true Vine, and we are the branches extending out of Him.

History and Destiny

As God's children, we must know who we are, where we have been, and where we are going. Every person, regardless of gender, race, or nationality, must find himself in the volume of the Book and fulfill God's predestined will for his life (Ps. 40:7; Heb. 10:7). Every generation must find its history and destiny in the Book. We must become like Jesus, the Pattern Son. He knew where He came from and where He was going; therefore, His present was never a problem.

The greatest enemy to faith and hope is an uncriticized present. We cannot remain comfortable where we are. We cannot remain confined within the comfort zones of our own prejudices, selfishly choosing whom we love. We must understand our history so that we can discover our manifold (many-sided) destiny. This is exampled by both the law and the prophets.

The law, the Torah, the first five books of the Bible, is a narrative, a story that was to be passed down from generation to generation. Jewish culture preserved this art of storytelling. Through retelling the story, the God who wrote the story would come into their telling of it and became as real to the people as though the events had just happened. The law was an energized memory. Something has to stretch us from the past. Someone has to go back and retell the story of the divine Seed, the seed of Abraham and David. We are energized by the memory of a God who moved in the past.

But that is not enough. We must then discover the prophets who constitute a radical hope. The majority of their writings was not a call for repentance but the declaration of a new thing coming. Thus we see the creation of the new thing through the articulation of faith from the mouths of those who believed.

So the law is an energized memory, the history of God's family. And the prophets are a radical hope, our destiny. Stirred by the past and stretched toward the future, our present becomes a place of creative truth in tension as we are driven by a resurrected memory into hope unseen.

We are sojourners like Abraham, who looked for a city, or a people, with foundations whose Builder and Maker is God (Heb. 11:10). If we lose sight of that energized memory or radical hope, we will become stagnant and comfortable where we are. The present world is not the world that shall be; therefore, we don't have to accept it for what it is now. We can rely on a collective memory of our history in the Book and by that memory be energized into the radical hope of something that doesn't yet exist; but it will!

Real hope breeds real faith. Though you live in conflict (the trial of your faith), you will find in God's Word by His Spirit the stamina to move on until you see the promise or until you see hope dawning in the next generation. That kind of faith is based upon the reality of who you are in Christ, not gender, race, or nationality. We must finish our course and fight the good fight of faith completely to the end—until we accomplish the purpose for which we were born. We must not depart prematurely from the arena of usefulness to God.

History has passed before us, and destiny lies ahead of us. We are part of a continuum and must find our own place in that ongoing, anointed purpose. Only then can we rest. We have been apprehended. God has tagged us and run, and we have been chasing Him ever since.

You will never get to where you want to be until you know why you are where you are. Even though we are born again, we were first born into a corrupt society with a corrupt government. The narrative of Exodus disdains Pharaoh. Redemption brings men to a place where they realize that there are those who are in power and authority who don't have a right to rule over them because they have rebelled against God. In the midst of such a society, God will bring forth a people, His elect family, whom He has destined for freedom and a new place of glory.

Faith does not evolve; faith is transformational. Transformation means to transcend the pattern or form. The only way we can transcend from one form to another is to break out of our present situation. Deliverance from prejudices of gender, race, and nationality will launch the Church into a new vision for the twenty-first century.

Life-changing faith is developed through crises and breaking points. It's not nice and smooth. When we satisfy His purpose in our current position, God breaks us out of it and disorients us away from it. He then brings us into the unfamiliar once again so we might lean on Him until it is time to enter new territory. For example, the truths contained in this volume regarding the public ministry of women, the rightful place for people of color, and the position of Jew and gentile alike before God will shake up old concepts and ideas. But real, transformational faith requires crisis, pressure, trouble, conflict, tribulation—these are the agents that metamorphose our faith.

The Greek word for "tribulation" means "pressure," and it conveys the picture of grapes being crushed in the winepress (see Mt. 13:21; Jn. 16:33; Acts 14:22; Rom. 5:3; 1 Thess. 3:4). Sometimes God puts the squeeze on the outer structure of what appears to be our vision to find out if there really is juice in there. Every ministry is feeling pressure right now. The Day of the Lord will declare the nature of every man's work. Transformation transcends the current form. The Church world is filled with prejudices based on gender, race, and nationality. We have gotten used to God meeting us in these old wineskins without ever realizing that He is bigger than that. Therefore God must shatter the old form.

As exampled by the potter's wheel, the Creator has deliberately allowed flaws in the vessel so that we will learn to depend on Him. Stay on the wheel where there is plenty of water to keep you pliable. If you take yourself off the wheel when you are marred, there won't be any water to keep you moist—you'll dry out and crack. But if the wheel is turning, and the hand is moving, depend on the One who made you afflicted, and there will be enough water to remake you into something new!

The Lord gives and the Lord takes away. We have entered a season in which what He has given has begun to weary us and no longer satisfies. He is now shaking and removing it, so that He might drive us into a new perspective. American Christians hate crises...we were built for comfort. But we must be delivered from prejudice, really changed. To live is to grow. To grow is to change, and spiritual growth denotes change after change after change (Ps. 84:7; Rom. 1:17; 2 Cor. 3:18).

The woman of Isaiah 54:1-5 (a picture of the Church) who will be the positional woman in the next move of God will always be the one who is barren. God constantly starts with the barren area (not the fruitful area) of your life and gives it a promise. God is currently showing us the sin of prejudice and the rotten fruit it has produced. Present things are not the way they ought to be. Unless we groan and grieve over the status quo, we will never be birthed into a new move of God. It will require an intercession born of the Holy Ghost where we feel the grieving of God over present situations that bind us to move us into our predetermined destiny.

As seen earlier, Jacob the schemer became Israel the prevailing prince. God taught him how to go up and down the ladder— accessing the secret place of the most high, perceiving the secrets of God, and seeing the generations to come. We, too, must meet God face to face and allow Him to smite the hollowness of our bigotry. Our thigh (the place of creativity and reproduction) must shrink, so that we will produce the seed of God, not the seed of human wisdom and strength. Only then can we really bless our children.

Eternal life is more than dying and going to Heaven. Eternal life is also when the next generation receives your spirit and continues in what God gave you. When Jesus died, He died childless. Jesus the Bridegroom had no kids. But Jesus is alive because the law of the kinsman Redeemer was in effect. When the older brother died without children, the next in line came and raised up seed to continue the family name. What the law could not do, Jesus did!

Jesus lives from generation to generation by the Holy Ghost! We have examined the sins of gender prejudice, racial prejudice, and national prejudice. We now know and understand that His seed is spiritual, having nothing to do with these natural issues and things. God's greatest hope is that He will have an anointed Family in the image of His firstborn Son. He shall see His seed, and they shall prolong His days.

The hour has come for Christ to be fully formed in His people. Jesus' experience on the Mount of Transfiguration is a panoramic expression of these days. This great event took place "after six days"(Mt. 17:1). We are living in the sixth day from Adam and the third day from Jesus (Hos. 6:1-3; Jn. 2:1; 2 Pet. 3:8). There on the mountain of glorious change Jesus experienced an energizing memory and a radical hope, for there He met with Moses who represented the law, and Elijah, who represented the prophets. These two men showed up that day for a purpose.

Lk. 9:30-31, KJV

And, behold, there talked with Him two men, which were Moses and Elias:

Who appeared in glory, and spake of His decease which He should accomplish at Jerusalem.

Moses came to teach Him how to *die*. The word "decease" is *exodos* and means "to go out, to depart." Elijah came to teach Him how to *live*, how to rise up in resurrection.

2 Kings 2:9-10, KJV

> *And it came to pass, when they were gone over, that Elijah said unto Elisha, Ask what I shall do for thee, before I be taken away from thee. And Elisha said, I pray thee, let a double portion of thy spirit be upon me.*
>
> *And he said, Thou hast asked a hard thing: nevertheless, if thou see me when I am taken from thee, it shall be so unto thee; but if not, it shall not be so.*

When Elijah ascended, his mantle, his anointing (a type of Christ) never left the planet. That anointing is ever increasing and being compounded exponentially. The river of Ezekiel 47 is rising! The only criterion for the young prophet to receive a "double portion," or "portion of the firstborn" of Elijah's "spirit" or "mouth" was that he see Elijah in his *going up*.

When Jesus ascended, His anointing remained in the earth to be administered by the coming of the Holy Ghost— Christ in each of us. The only criterion for us, His seed, to prolong His days and ministry, is to perceive Him in His *ascension* and *coronation*!

Our evangelical and Pentecostal roots never emphasized the enthroned Christ. He is not our soon-coming King. He is King now! To behold the transcendent One in His going up will deliver us from all prejudice. To see Him as He *is* will save us from seeing male and female, black and white, Jew and Greek. To acknowledge the risen and exalted Christ will enable us to sit, walk, and stand with Him in heavenly places. To grasp His more excellent ministry will enable us to participate in the word and ministry of reconciliation; we are His end-time ambassadors and dispensers of the New Covenant, the good news that Jesus died and rose again for all, men and women of every race and nation!

Gal. 3:26-29, NIV

You are all sons of God through faith in Christ Jesus,

for all of you who were baptized into Christ have clothed yourselves with Christ.

There is neither Jew nor Greek, slave nor free, male nor female, for you are all one in Christ Jesus.

If you belong to Christ, then you are Abraham's seed, and heirs according to the promise.

Eph. 1:9-10, AMP

Making known to us the mystery (secret) of His will (of His plan, of His purpose). [And it is this:] In accordance with His good pleasure (His merciful intention) which He had previously purposed and set forth in Him,

[He planned] for the maturity of the times and the climax of the ages to unify all things and head them up and consummate them in Christ, [both] things in heaven and things on the earth.

We have reached the maturity of the times. God is sending the divine reed of His Word to measure His worshipers and their worship.

Rev. 11:1, KJV

And there was given me a reed like unto a rod: and the angel stood, saying, Rise, and measure the temple of God, and the altar, and them that worship therein.

How wide are you? What is the scope of your spiritual breadth? How big is your mercy? Will you walk with your brothers and sisters, or will you continue to pick those whom you love and serve?

How long are you? Is there a preconceived or predetermined limit to your spiritual length? How stretched is your endurance? Are you still politicking and patty-caking with the three prejudices, playing games with the call of God, or have you made the commitment to ascend all the way to Zion's summit with God and all His people?

To all who hear this word—male and female, black and white, Jew and Greek—I beseech you by His grace, can we finally accept each other in Christ? And once we do, will we let His love take us to His full stature?

Prejudice in any form is the innate, corrupted character of the old Adamic nature that causes men to choose whom they love. Such discrimination has to do with character— the heart condition of the inner man. Our only hope, the only lasting cure for this unrighteousness in the Church and in our society is the supernatural, unconditional love of God poured out upon us by the Holy Spirit. Let us pray and turn from our wicked ways. He will forgive us and heal our land (2 Chron. 7:14).

Revival fires are breaking forth throughout the earth. This generation cannot afford to miss its critical time of visitation. Our petty prejudices can no longer be allowed to grieve His Holy Spirit.

Arise and shine, for your light has come. As true worshipers, let men and women, people of every race and nation, begin to exalt Jesus Christ as Lord of all.

We have yet to sing the kind of song we are capable of singing— together.

Endnotes

Preface

1. Jean McKechnie, ed., *Webster's New Universal Unabridged Dictionary* (Cleveland, OH: Dorset & Baber, 1983), 1420.

Chapter 1

1. This truth is thoroughly expressed in Chapter One of my book, *The Time of the Messiah* (Shippensburg, PA: Destiny Image, 1996).

2. Chapter Seven of my book, *The More Excellent Ministry* (Shippensburg, PA: Destiny Image, 1988), and Chapter Three of my book, *The Priesthood Is Changing* (Shippensburg, PA: Destiny Image, 1991) explain the historical setting and meaning of these two covenants in fuller detail.

3. Joseph Henry Thayer, *The New Thayer's Greek-English Lexicon of the New Testament* (Lafayette, IN, n.d.), 317.

4. Geoffrey W. Bromiley, ed., *"Little Kittel" Theological Dictionary of the New Testament* (Grand Rapids, MI: William B. Eerdmans Publishing Company, 1988), 388.

Chapter 2

1. For more on this, see Chapter Two of my book, *The More Excellent Ministry,* entitled, "A Ministry Without Condemnation" (Shippensburg, PA: Destiny Image, 1988).

Chapter 3

1. John R. Rice, *Bobbed Hair, Bossy Wives, and Women Preachers* (Wheaton, IL: Sword of the Lord Publishers, 1941), 78-79.

2. *Matthew Henry's Commentary,* vol. 1 (Marshallton, DE: The National Foundation for Christian Education, n.d.), 12.

Chapter 4

1. *The Homilies of St. John Chrysostom, Nicene and Post-Nicene Fathers, Series I* (Grand Rapids, MI: Eerdmans Publishing, 1956).

2. *Greek-English Lexicon of the New Testament* (Grand Rapids, MI: Zondervan, 1968), 306.

3. Leonard Swidler, *Biblical Affirmations of Women* (Philadelphia, PA: Westminster Press, 1979), 299.

Chapter 5

1. Swidler, *Biblical Affirmations,* 342.

2. George Tavard, *Women in Christian Tradition* (South Bend, IN: University of Notre Dame Press, 1973), 68.

3. Leonard Swidler, *Biblical Affirmations*, 346.

4. *Patrologia Latina*, vol. 17., Col. 253 (New York, NY: Adlers Foreign Books).

5. *The Ante-Nicene Fathers*, vol. 7 (Grand Rapids, MI: Eerdmans Publishing, 1985), 431.

6. Swidler, *Biblical Affirmations*, 314.

7. Swidler, *Biblical Affirmations*, 314.

8. Taken from "Women in the Early Church" and "Women in the Medieval Church," *Christian History*, vol. VII, no. 1, issue 17 (Worchester, PA, 1994), 1-38.

9. Taken from Edith Deen, *Great Women of the Christian Faith* (New York: Harper and Brothers Publishers, 1959).

10. Maria Woodworth-Etter, *Diary of Signs and Wonders* (Tulsa, OK: Harrison House, 1916).

11. Taken from Stanley Burgess and Gary McGee, *The Dictionary of Pentecostal and Charismatic Movements* (Grand Rapids, MI: Zondervan Publishing House, 1988).

12. Kathryn Kuhlman, *I Believe in Miracles* (Old Tappan, NJ: Fleming H. Revell Co., 1962).

Chapter 6

1. Katherine C. Bushnell, *God's Word to Women* (Mossville, IL: God's Word to Women Publishers, 1923), 360-361.

2. Ruth A. Tucker and Walter L. Liefeld, *Daughters of the Church* (Grand Rapids, MI: Zondervan Publishing House, 1987), 441.

Chapter 7

1. Emmanuel Johnson, *I'm Not Black, You're Not White* Shippensburg, PA: Destiny Image Publishers, 1990).

2. Luther Blackwell, *The Heritage of the Black Believer* (Shippensburg, PA: Treasure House Publishers, 1993), 53-54.

3. Wayne Perryman, *The 1993 Trial on the Curse of Ham* (Bakersfield, CA: Pneuma Life Publishing, 1994), 26-31.

4. Jefferson Edwards, *Gifted* (Bakersfield, CA: Pneuma Life Publishing, 1994), 42.

5. Dr. Ronald Washington, *Forgiveness and Reconciliation* (Shippensburg, PA: Treasure House, 1993), 13.

Chapter 8

1. Bishop Alfred G. Dunston, Jr., *The Black Man in the Old Testament* (Trenton, NJ: Africa World Press, 1992), X.

2. William Dwight McKissic, Sr., *Beyond Roots* (Wenonah, NJ: Renaissance Productions, 1990), 52.

3. John L. Johnson *The Black Biblical Heritage* (Nashville, TN: Winston-Derek Publishers, Inc., 1991), 230.

4. Johnson, *Black Biblical Heritage*, 79, 83, 107-108.

5. Jefferson Edwards, *Chosen, Not Cursed* (Tulsa, OK: Vincom, 1989), 51.

6. Carlisle John Peterson, *The Destiny of the Black Race* (Toronto, ON: Lifeline Communications, 1991), 239-242.

7. McKissic, *Beyond Roots*, 37.

8. McKissic, *Beyond Roots*, 38.

9. Johnson, *I'm Not Black*, 93-94.

10. *The Holy Bible, Black Heritage Edition* (Nashville, TN: Today, Inc., 1976).

11. James M. Washington, ed., *A Testament of Hope, The Essential Writings of Martin Luther King, Jr.* (San Francisco, CA: Harper & Row Publishers, 1986), 219.

12. Taken from the cover of Rachel Kranz, *The Biographical Dictionary of Black Americans* (New York, NY: Facts on File, Inc., 1992).

13. Lerone Bennett, Jr., *Great Moments in Black History* (Chicago, IL: Johnson Publishing Co., 1992), 79-94.

14. Stanley M. Burgess and Gary B. McGee, ed., *Dictionary of Pentecostal and Charismatic Movement*, 77-86.

Chapter 9

1. Luther Blackwell, *The Heritage*, 115.

2. Edwards, *Chosen, Not Cursed*, 3-4.

3. Michael Goings, *Free at Last?* (Shippensburg, PA: Treasure House, 1995), 79-95.

4. Goings, *Free at Last*, 97.

Chapter 10

1. Michael Brown, *Our Hands Are Stained With Blood* (Shippensburg, PA: Destiny Image, 1992), 86-87.

2. Brown, *Our Hands Are Stained*, 134.

3. The reader is encouraged to study the blessings and the cursings of the remainder of Deuteronomy 30. Note that verses 11-14 regarding the "word" of faith are restated by the apostle Paul in Romans 10:6-10.

Chapter 11

1. Thayer, *The New Thayer's Greek-English Lexicon*.

2. Brown, *Our Hands Are Stained*, 138.

Books & Tapes by Kelley Varner

TAPE CATALOG

To receive a full listing of Pastor Varner's books and tapes, write or call for our current catalog:

Praise Tabernacle
P.O. Box 785
Richlands, NC 28574-0785
(910) 324-5026 or 324-5027
FAX: (910) 324-1048
E-mail: kvarner@nternet.net OR
Kvarner@templebuilders.com
Internet: http://www.reapernet.com OR
http://www.templebuilders.com

TAPE OF THE MONTH

Each month two cassette tapes are made available by Pastor Varner. These messages are ministered by him and others in the fivefold ministry. You may join this growing list of listeners on a monthly offering basis.

VIDEO CASSETTES

We are just beginning this new avenue of ministry. Presently available are three, two-hour video cassettes on the Book of Ruth. This teaching is a verse-by-verse exegesis concerning the Christian walk from conception to perfection, from birth to maturity. Please write or call for more information.

SEMINARS AND CONVENTIONS

There are annual meetings here in Richlands for the Body of Christ. Please inquire for information on the next meeting. There is a team of ministry here at Praise Tabernacle that is available to your local church to teach the principles of restoration and assist in the areas of praise and worship. Please contact Pastor Varner.

Other exciting titles by Kelley Varner

PREVAIL—A HANDBOOK FOR THE OVERCOMER
ISBN 0-938612-06-9 $10.99p

THE MORE EXCELLENT MINISTRY
ISBN 0-914903-60-8 $10.99p

THE PRIESTHOOD IS CHANGING
ISBN 1-56043-033-8 $10.99p

Are you committed to growing in God? Are you seeking greater fulfillment in your relationship with Him? Don't miss any one of these three books! Their message can change your life!

UNDERSTANDING TYPES, SHADOWS & NAMES, VOLS. 1 & 2
The first two volumes in a series, they examine the main definition of a biblical term, its themes, how Christ fulfilled it, and how it applies to Christianity.
Vol. 1 ISBN 1-56043-165-2 $16.99c   Vol. 2 ISBN 1-56043-197-0 $16.99c

WHOSE RIGHT IT IS
Here Pastor Varner carefully examines the Scriptures for a proper perspective on Christ's Lordship and dispensationalism.
ISBN 1-56043-151-2 $10.99p

REST IN THE DAY OF TROUBLE
This book studies in detail the prophecy of Habakkuk. We too are in a day of trouble and, like Habakkuk, can we find rest in ours?
ISBN 1-56043-119-9 $10.99p

UNSHAKEABLE PEACE
In a detailed study of the Book of Haggai, Pastor Varner presents the *unshakeable peace* that characterizes the Church that Jesus is building!
ISBN 1-56043-137-7 $10.99p

THE TIME OF THE MESSIAH
There are four characteristics of the Messiah's first coming. Can you recognize these same signs in our present season—the season of the Holy Spirit upon the Church?
ISBN 1-56043-177-6 $10.99p

CORPORATE ANOINTING
Just as a united front is more powerful in battle, so is the anointing when Christians come together in unity! Learn how God longs to reveal the fullness of Christ in the fullness of His Body in power and glory.
ISBN 0-7684-2011-3 $10.99p

Available at your local Christian bookstore.

Internet: http://www.reapernet.com

D *Destiny Image*
New Releases

AUDIENCE OF ONE
by Jeremy and Connie Sinnott.
More than just a book about worship, *Audience of One* will lead you into experiencing intimacy and love for the only One who matters—your heavenly Father. Worship leaders and associate pastors themselves, Jeremy and Connie Sinnott have been on a journey of discovering true spiritual worship for years. Then they found a whole new dimension to worship—its passion, intimacy, and love for the Father, your *audience of One*.
ISBN 0-7684-2014-8 $10.99p

THE HIDDEN POWER OF PRAYER AND FASTING
by Mahesh Chavda.
How do you react when overwhelming defeat stares you in the eye? What do you do when faced with insurmountable odds? God has provided a way to turn certain defeat into awesome victory—through prayer and fasting! An international evangelist and the senior pastor of All Nations Church in Charlotte, North Carolina, Mahesh Chavda has seen firsthand the power of God released through a lifestyle of prayer and fasting. Here he shares from decades of personal experience and scriptural study principles and practical tips about fasting and praying. This book will inspire you to tap into God's power and change your life, your city, and your nation!
ISBN 0-7684-2017-2 $10.99p

THE GOD CHASERS
by Tommy Tenney.
Are you dissatisfied with "church"? Are you looking for more? Do you yearn to touch God? You may be a *God chaser*! The passion of Tommy Tenney, evangelist and third-generation Pentecostal minister, is to "catch" God and find himself in God's manifest presence. For too long God's children have been content with crumbs. The Father is looking for those who will seek His face. This book will enflame your own desire to seek God with your whole heart and being—and to find Him.
ISBN 0-7684-2016-4 $11.99p

THE LOST ART OF INTERCESSION
by Jim W. Goll.
The founder of Ministry to the Nations, Jim Goll has traveled the world in a teaching and prophetic ministry. All over the globe God is moving—He is responding to the prayers of His people. Here Jim Goll teaches the lessons learned by the Moravians during their 100-year prayer Watch. They sent up prayers; God sent down His power. Through Scripture, the Moravian example, and his own prayer life, Jim Goll proves that "what goes up must come down."
ISBN 1-56043-697-2 $10.99p

Available at your local Christian bookstore.

Internet: http://www.reapernet.com

Prices subject to change without notice.   5:10

Other
Destiny Image titles
you will enjoy reading

NON-RELIGIOUS CHRISTIANITY
by Gerald Coates.
If Jesus Christ returned today, how much of "church" would He condone or condemn? In this book, Gerald Coates contends that "religion" is the greatest hindrance to making Jesus attractive to our family, neighbors, and co-workers. Humorous yet confrontational, this popular British speaker and church leader will surprise you with his conclusions. This book could change your life forever!
ISBN 1-56043-694-8 $10.99p

ENCOUNTERING THE PRESENCE
by Colin Urquhart.
What is it about Jesus that, when we encounter Him, we are changed? When we encounter the Presence, we encounter the Truth, because Jesus is the Truth. Here Colin Urquhart, best-selling author and pastor in Sussex, England, explains how the Truth changes facts. Do you desire to become more like Jesus? The Truth will set you free!
ISBN 0-7684-2018-0 $10.99p

ANOINTED OR ANNOYING?
by Ken Gott.
Don't miss out on the powerful move of God that is in the earth today! When you encounter God's Presence in revival, you have a choice—accept it or reject it; become anointed or annoying! Ken Gott, former pastor of Sunderland Christian Centre and now head of Revival Now! International Ministries, calls you to examine your own heart and motives for pursuing God's anointing, and challenges you to walk a life of obedience!
ISBN 0-7684-1003-7 $10.99p

Available at your local Christian bookstore.

Internet: http://www.reapernet.com

Prices subject to change without notice.   4:1

Exciting titles by Don Nori

THE POWER OF BROKENNESS

Accepting Brokenness is a must for becoming a true vessel of the Lord, and is a stepping-stone to revival in our hearts, our homes, and our churches. Brokenness alone brings us to the wonderful revelation of how deep and great our Lord's mercy really is. Join this companion who leads us through the darkest of nights. Discover the *Power of Brokenness*.
ISBN 1-56043-178-4 $10.99p

THE ANGEL AND THE JUDGMENT

Few understand the power of our judgments—or the aftermath of the words we speak in thoughtless, emotional pain. In this powerful story about a preacher and an angel, you'll see how the heavens respond and how the earth is changed by the words we utter in secret.
ISBN 1-56043-154-7 $11.99p

HIS MANIFEST PRESENCE

This is a passionate look at God's desire for a people with whom He can have intimate fellowship. Not simply a book on worship, it faces our triumphs as well as our sorrows in relation to God's plan for a dwelling place that is splendid in holiness and love.
ISBN 0-914903-48-9 $10.99p
Also available in Spanish.
ISBN 1-56043-079-6 $10.99p

SECRETS OF THE MOST HOLY PLACE

Here is a prophetic parable you will read again and again. The winds of God are blowing, drawing you to His Life within the Veil of the Most Holy Place. There you begin to see as you experience a depth of relationship your heart has yearned for. This book is a living, dynamic experience with God!
ISBN 1-56043-076-1 $10.99p

Available at your local Christian bookstore.

Internet: http://www.reapernet.com

Prices subject to change without notice.   4:38

Exciting titles
by Mark Hanby

ANOINTING THE UNSANCTIFIED
The anointing is more than a talented performance or an emotional response. In this book, Dr. Hanby details the essential ingredients of directional relationship that allow the Spirit of God to flow down upon the Body of Christ—and from us to the needs of a dying world.
ISBN 1-56043-071-0 $10.99p

THE HOUSE THAT GOD BUILT
Beyond whatever man can desire is a God-given pattern for the life of the Church. Here Dr. Hanby unfolds practical applications from the design of the Tabernacle that allow us to become the house God is building today.
ISBN 1-56043-091-5 $9.99p

PERCEIVING THE WHEEL OF GOD
On the potter's wheel, a lump of clay yields to a necessary process of careful pressure and constant twisting. Similarly, the form of true faith is shaped by a trusting response to the hand of God in a suffering situation. This book offers essential understanding for victory through the struggles of life.
ISBN 1-56043-109-1 $9.99p

THE RENEWING OF THE HOLY GHOST
Do you need renewal? Everything in the natural, from birds to blood cells, must either undergo a process of renewal or enter into death. Our spiritual life is no different. With this book, your renewal can begin today!
ISBN 1-56043-031-1 $6.99p

YOU HAVE NOT MANY FATHERS
by Dr. Mark Hanby with Craig Ervin.
Explore with Dr. Hanby the relationship of father and son as the foundational connection for all spiritual impartation. As we turn our hearts toward one another, we will recover our heritage of generational blessing and double-portion anointing!
ISBN 1-56043-166-0 $10.99p

Available at your local Christian bookstore.
Internet: http://www.reapernet.com

Other
Destiny Image titles
you will enjoy reading

RIGHT OR RECONCILED?
by Joseph L. Garlington.
The message of reconciliation that the Church must declare is simple yet profound: "God is not holding your sins against you!" This is the belief of Joseph L. Garlington, Sr., pastor of a large multiracial congregation in Pittsburgh. Whether you are concerned about racial, gender, or denominational reconciliation, this book is for you. You will never see reconciliation in the same light again!
ISBN 0-7684-2004-0 $10.99p

ONE BLOOD
by Earl Paulk.
Step into the shoes of a man who dared to "rock the boat" by taking part in the civil rights movement deep in the heart of the South. Read in this book the astounding story of Earl Paulk's commitment to a Church in which every member is of "one blood" and one Spirit. See from a unique, inside perspective some of the greatest civil rights leaders of the century. A must-read book!
ISBN 1-56043-175-X $12.99p

RELEASERS OF LIFE
by Mary Audrey Raycroft.
Inside you is a river that is waiting to be tapped—the river of the Holy Spirit and power! Let Mary Audrey Raycroft, a gifted exhorter and teacher and the Pastor of Equipping Ministries and Women in Ministry at the Toronto Airport Christian Fellowship, teach you how you can release the unique gifts and anointings that the Lord has placed within you. Discover how you can move and minister in God's freeing power and be a releaser of life!
ISBN 1-56043-198-9 $10.99p

OUR HANDS ARE STAINED WITH BLOOD
by Dr. Michael L. Brown.
From the first "Christian" persecutions of the Jews in the fourth century to the horrors of the Holocaust, from Israel-bashing in today's press to anti-Semitism in today's pulpits, this shocking and painful book tells the tragic story that every Christian must hear.
ISBN 1-56043-068-0 $10.99p

Available at your local Christian bookstore.

Internet: http://www.reapernet.com

Prices subject to change without notice.   5:24